C O N T E N T S

EDINBUR E 99

Edinburgh Review
22a Buccleuch Place Edinburgh EH8 9LN
tel/fax 0131-651 1415

co-editors Sophy Dale
Robert Alan Jamieson
advisory editor Alec Finlay
cover Alex Thomson, Sophy Dale
production Pam O'Connor
logo Alasdair Gray
cover image Francesca Hetherington

ISSN 0267 6672 ISBN 0 7486 13064

distributed in the UK by Edinburgh University Press
typeset in Sabon by Koinonia Ltd, Bury
printed and bound in Great Britain by
by Page Bros Limited, Norwich

subsidised by the THE SCOTTISH ARTS COUNCIL

back issues available
from Edinburgh University Press
22 George Square,
Edinburgh EH8 9LF
tel 0131-650 6206

'ends and beginnings'

THE OLD POET

Before I go over the horizon of the dark
let me do my last poetry reading in a hall
where there are no excuses from the chairman
and the room is full of fragrance. And people cry
to think of their bones shining towards evening.
And the hall is crammed with leafy presences,
the dead, the living, and all who were friends to me
when I grew up in the hot mists of June.
And like Eurydice I'll say farewell to them
as I'm gathered to the shades in the lyre's sound
and the steps climb steadily towards a daylight
which I shall never see as my wings fold.

IAIN CRICHTON SMITH (1928-98)

THE DAY OF WRITING is the day of Iain Crichton Smith's funeral. A grey dawning and a chill wind, a stark clarity in the cold air as the light rises. The seamaws are all offshore. The water is warmer than the land this morning.

These last two or three years, which have brought the passing of such as Jessie Kesson, Sorley Maclean, Norman MacCaig, Tom Scott (whose translation of Pasolini's 'Le Litanie del bel Ragazzo' is included in this issue), George Mackay Brown and now ICS, seem to demonstrate the Ecclesiastical truth, that dying too has its season. No wonder if our heads bow down, bereaved of elders. The loss of these writers who have spanned the late Empire to the dawn of Devolution, covering among them the better part of this muckle wee country, is a sair wound. On the literary map of Scotland, where once these were beacons, there are fewer lights and fewer. This latest death gusts out of a gale.

Never writers to illuminate the top of the bestsellers' list, they demonstrate perfectly the invalidity of the in-vogue commerce-led culture of the free-marketeers. All were what ICS's Murdo might have called 'literary-crofters', in the sense that their writing was for long enough subsidised by other incomes. And all were in their way teachers, encouragers of younger writers in the best traditions of the dominie. They understood the value of 'creative' writing not as a commodity to be bought and sold, but as a medium for personal development. They understood the importance of literature through the direct action of education.

By sad coincidence we publish here a major interview between Mario Relich and Iain Crichton Smith, conducted in the last spring of his life. Reading through this text now, the loss is plain – loss not merely to Scottish but to world culture – of a mind at ease with itself, a sage who had long since reached his zen enlightenment.

In the light of this, and considering *Edinburgh Review 99* is the first issue from its new/old home in Buccleuch Place, and the last of its first century, the title of ICS's recent volume *Ends and Beginnings* seems an appropriate one for this editorial – that volume of post-'collected' poems which carried us beyond assumed conclusion, beyond the midnight dark to the first streaks of dawn, as Iain himself, a Ne'erday wean, bridged old to new.

'Ends and beginnings' describes well how it feels, this 19(99) mood, as we all go 'over the horizon of the dark'. The growth of the passing season dies back, leaves begin to gather on the ground, and it's easy to focus only on the 'ends' – these leaves gave us the very air we breathe. But where history is ending, we must see beyond 'the end', remember how dying vegetation feeds the coming growth – implicit in Patrick Geddes' biosophic motto, 'By Leaves We Live', is the shedding time.

TRANSLATIONS: ALTERED STATES

The sense of wholeness, seeing shedding and budding contained one within the other which informs Geddes' notion of biosophy, finds echoes in the concern with the setting of culture in its context of nature which is clearly to be seen in Peter McCarey's essay in this volume, 'Find an Angel and pick a Fight', or in the pieces by Gerrie Fellows and Coral Hull. Indeed, the concept of biosophy would seem to fit in well with Edinburgh Review's motto, 'to gather all the rays of culture into one'.

Whilst this issue of the magazine pays tribute to the passing of Iain Crichton Smith's voice, it also gives space to new growth, in the voices of emerging writers from Scotland and around the world. At the same time, old roots are explored in the new translations by Peter Constantine of poems from the oral tradition of the Arvanites, Brian Holton's translations of the thirteenth-century Chinese poet Qiao Jifu and Andrew Schelling's translations of poems from the *Sattasi* of King Hala, which pre-date the earliest verses from classical Sanskrit.

This issue of *Edinburgh Review* is more than usually concerned with the notion of translation – partly as a result of the significant number of pieces originally written in a language other than English, the four-way translations in Italian, Friulian, English and Scots of Pasolini's poetry being a notable example; but also explicitly discussed in pieces such as Kaarina Hollo's interview with Nuala ní Dhomhnaill on the politics and pitfalls of translation. Translation further exists as an underlying theme in pieces such as Gerrie Fellows' 'Counterpoints', in which place and memory contain the translated voices both of Maoris and of white settlers in 'Godzone' New Zealand, whilst Coral Hull's 'Taronga Park Zoo' and 'Bronx Zoo' depict the most brutal of translations, animals wrenched out of their own contexts and forced into the unnatural state of the zoo.

The appearance of John Burnside's 'Ether' and Stuart Hood's translation of Dario Fo, 'The Resurrection of Lazarus' in this issue might allow for the raising of Lazarus from the dead to be transformed into a metaphor for the relationship between translation and 'minority' languages such as Friulian, Arvanitka or Gaelic: allowing poems to come alive to a new world-wide English-speaking audience. As ní Dhomhnaill points out, translation involves a two-way traffic, and not all its implications are straightforwardly positive with regard to minority languages. However, her contention that translation allows a way in to poems for readers who would otherwise be 'disenfranchised' by their lack of a language, and her celebration of the fact that 'every translation is first of all an enormously careful act of reading, and you really have to give the reader his/her due as well' suggests both the care and craft which go into translation, and the creative force which the act of translation contains. Translation encompasses ends and beginnings; shedding the words of the original piece in order to allow for the growth in their place of new words in a different language. These new words form a poem or story which is at once new and not-new: the same poem or story, but in an altered state.

STORIES

JOHN BURNSIDE

ZIRANNA ZATELI

REGI CLAIRE

DARIO FO / STUART HOOD

Ether

John Burnside

ON SUNDAYS WE would drive home in the dark, past the quarry and the black woods, our headlamps sweeping over fields of swede or kale, then beaming out into the darkness. Sometimes my mother would tell stories; sometimes she'd just talk about things, like how our lights would go on travelling into space, and never stop. I liked the idea of that but I never believed her. I would fall asleep for minutes at a time, then wake as we reached the first house lights on Grafton Road; from there, I would follow our route all the way home: past the graveyard threaded with mist or smoke in the orange light; past the empty playgrounds of my school, one for the girls and one for the boys; past the church; past Brewster's Newsagents and Tobacconists. I knew every door and gatepost on our street. I knew whose lights would be on, the light in the hall, or the light in the kitchen, and I loved those pale, goldish lights from upstairs, that always look warmer when you're on the outside. It made me feel good to think that every house had its own story, unwinding behind each window like a slow, mysterious film. I didn't want there to be any gaps. I remember when I first heard about the ether, how people had to believe in it once, because they didn't think light could travel through emptiness. For a long time after I knew they were wrong, I still believed they were right. It might not be true, but it was a better story, and that was what really mattered.

*

My childhood was a series of doubtful stories. I would hear them from my mother and her friends; I would hear them in church, or read them in the Sunday papers; when my mother gave me a radio to keep in my room, I would tune in to tales of mayhem or terror, of haunted houses and ghastly murders that made my hair stand on end with delight. The thing was, all these accounts were supposed to be true. Or rather, unless the teller claimed some grounding in history, however slight, the stories meant nothing to me, and were soon forgotten. I remember one I heard, where a boy went out to fetch water from the stream in some remote northern settlement. When he didn't return his parents went looking for him, but all they found was the abandoned bucket, and a trail of crisp new prints in the snow that vanished into thin air, twenty feet from the water's edge. There was no sign of a struggle, no evidence to suggest someone else had been there and, on that still winter's day, when a dog's bark would carry from one parish to another, they'd heard no sound, no cry for help. For weeks afterwards, whenever I was sent out for coal, I would listen as I crossed the yard, expecting some winged creature to emerge from the white stare of the snow. I'd walk out to the pool in the woods and gaze into its depths where, leaf-black and still, the ancient drowned lay buried in mud, half-decayed, their skins partly-tanned, their faces etched with the patterns of crowfoot and willow leaves.

*

Now all I want to do is to tell one story of my own. It won't be my story, as such; it will be more or less fictional, something that begins in the world, but ends up somewhere else, as an entirely mental event. Of course, if I could, I would write a whole book of stories, full of people like me, hoping for a different life, a state of grace, a cleaner way of being. I won't ever do it, though. I know my limitations. It may be that I choose them. Anyway, perhaps one story is enough.

Nevertheless, I would like to tell one story before it's too late. All I need is a space in the mind; a beginning, a middle and an end. Ideally, the story I tell will suggest a cleaner world – no less complex, no less subtle, just a world without the inevitable clouding of daily existence. I will tell my one story in winter, on the first day snow falls: I will sit by the window and say what I have to say, perhaps to a tape recorder, perhaps to an empty room. I may never write it down: the story might simply happen, as snow happens. I've always felt, watching snow, that what I'm watching is time. It's not like watching a clock: that's entirely artificial, an analogue; even if you remove the cover and gaze at the wheels and springs, all you see is a regular, contrived movement. Snow, on the other hand, is real time. The same flake never falls twice; no two are alike. The patterns are always changing. It's difficult to tell reality from illusion. In fanciful moments, I think of this as a representation of eternity, in the most perishable form possible. For personal reasons, I've been preoccupied with death all my life, which means I have also been preoccupied with eternity. You can't think about one without the other. I know there is something eternal in the world, but I wouldn't want to hazard a guess as to its nature.

That's why the story I will tell is only a variation on one that's already been told. I've considered others but, in the end, none of them works for me. For example, I've rejected the story of the exhumation of Thomas a Kempis. It defies belief that the man who wrote *The Imitation of Christ* was buried alive, then found, years later, his body twisted and wizened, the arms curled up under the coffin lid, each fingertip a robin's pincushion of splinters and old blood, where he'd scratched and clawed at the wood in his desperation. The irony is too obvious. Besides, I want my story to contain a resurrection of sorts: a small but significant triumph.

I am even tempted to repeat the story I heard from Silvia, one of my mother's friends, who had once lived in Italy – a story at once fanciful and everyday, concerning an old woman who had invited her to stay for a while at her country home. Silvia had been a sickly child, though by the time I knew her, she appeared in good health. The old woman, who had a great deal of money and no children of her own, had decided to more or less adopt Silvia and, for a whole summer, allowed her full run of the house and garden. The only place that was out of bounds was an old, dilapidated glasshouse, considered dangerous by Silvia's benefactor and, because it was forbidden, the ruin held a powerful fascination for a lonely child. She knew that every forbidden place has a story to tell – a dead lover, a ghostly woman, a murdered baby.

One afternoon, while the rest of the world was asleep, Silvia found a way into the ruined glasshouse and picked her way carefully through the litter of old clay pots and glass shards in the half-darkness within. The roof still hung with overgrown vines and wild trails of jasmine but, as her eyes became accustomed to the shadows, Silvia began to notice that, along one wall, in a neatly-ordered row, several dogs lay, as if sleeping, with their muzzles turned up, to scent the air in their hunters' dreams, and their paws outstretched, the way her mother's dog slept at home, quite motionless, tensed and expectant. She always laughed at herself when she told how long it had taken her to see that the dogs were not sleeping at all, that their still bodies were dead and mummified, the eyes covered with coins, the skins dry as parchment. She ran from the place in horror then, cutting her hand on a piece of glass; the first person she met was the old lady, who took her back to the house and got her to calm down. The next day Silvia was sent to the priest, to make her confession, and nothing more was said. Silvia used to say she still had dreams about those dogs. That's why this story belongs to her still and, besides, it suggests nothing more than death's stillness, and the story I want to tell must contain a resurrection. It has to be something familiar, something I know – perhaps it's nothing more than an atmosphere: a crispness in the air, like the space over a football pitch in autumn, drifts of copper leaves, echoes, a strangeness in the wind when it touches my face, reaching out from some unimaginable distance. It has to be one of the first stories I ever heard, the one I had suspected all along. The story I want to tell is this: that, beyond the rain, beyond the fields, beyond the fuzz of snow on the kitchen window, Lazarus is still in the tomb, waiting for someone to call him out, waiting to wake again.

*

Several versions of the Lazarus story are possible. The first, and most obvious, is a waking body, dusted with ice, breathing and moving again, returned to the living and, at the same time, suspended, like a foetus in a jar, perfectly preserved, in an odourless, colourless medium. This was the version I wanted to believe, the story in the textbooks. I could picture Lazarus as he was, raised to a world of cuttlefish and bees, to foreign utensils and food he could no longer stomach. Or I could imagine him at night, when his sisters were sleeping – the midnight feasts of sugars and tainted meat, bowls filled with elvers, oysters sucked from their shells. It was difficult to shrug off this image of a resurrected body: the slow and painful unwinding of the bandages, the whitish mycelium of pus and sweat on the skin and the first hint of decay: a bruised look, the blood that had been still for days only just beginning to quicken. In this resurrection, the dead man's eyes have already clouded; it will be weeks before the numbness seeps away through his fingers and, with it, the sweet comfort of inertia. It was an effort to replace this image with another, simpler idea: a deliberate heresy in which Lazarus is alone in a white interior lit with candles, rehearsing his own death and rising again – lying still for three days, listening, suspended in the heat. Like anything else, resurrection would require practice. Many died and did not return. Lazarus was caught in the space between death and rebirth and had to be drawn back home by Jesus. In one version of the story, he does not come back, but remains, beguiled by the silence, or by the music he thinks he can hear beyond the grave, and the one who returns in his place, though he resembles Lazarus outwardly in every respect is, in fact, his antithesis.

*

There was a story my mother would tell, about a spirit who lived under the duckweed on green ponds. She told it often; I suppose she wanted to protect me from the drowning or mutilation in the woods that seemed, at times, my inevitable destiny, but all I remembered were the exquisite details: a wrinkled bone-and-hair fiend that I wanted to exist in the black water; a gnarled hand deep in the mud; a black mouth rising to kiss or devour through the thin panes of leaves and ice. I imagined this creature as near-hermaphrodite, part-man, part-woman, part-toad, wired into the sway of the water, aware of the smallest ripple. It possessed an acute, fishlike sensitivity, where even rainfall is a tapping at the spine, but it knew the difference between ordinary disturbances of the surface and the paddling motion of a child's arm or a thrust stick. It had a name, I remember: it was called Jenny Greenteeth when it surged from the water, its long nails and jagged fangs coated with weed and moss. Quick as a pike, it would snap up its prey and disappear into the depths. There would be no struggle. A mocking stillness would return to the pond as the last ripples died away; birds would sing again while the bones were sucked empty below.

My mother is dead now. Somebody found her slumped in her seat, on the bus to the hospital, with a box of chocolates and a bouquet of flowers in her lap. It was a warm summer's afternoon, and she had slipped away like the woman in a fairy story who steps out of the light for a moment, into the shade of a hedge, where the dark weeds gather like messengers from a further world. The flowers were from our garden: tired roses and lupins wrapped in newspaper. After she was buried, I would go to the graveyard and lie beside her stone, with my head pressed to the ground, listening. I was terrified that she was still alive down there, with six feet of earth holding her down, scratching and crying out, where nobody could hear, like Thomas a Kempis.

*

During the last days, when Lazarus is alone in his dying and even his sisters have receded into the surprising depths of the sick room, he dreams several times that he is standing in an empty place, like the room in the temple outside the Holy of Holies, which no one is permitted to enter. There is a veil in this room and behind the veil is a light – the only light he sees in the dream, shining through the thin, almost transparent fabric. This light is close, but it is not local: Lazarus knows it extends beyond the veil in every direction – his impression is of something boundless. What is local is a figure, a form like his own, sometimes beyond the veil, enlarged by distance, sometimes so close that the material clings to its face and hands when it presses forward as if to push through and enter the cool room where Lazarus stands, fascinated. This figure resembles him, but in the dream he knows it is not Lazarus: it is a life that would assume any form in order to exist.

When he wakes, there are women around the bed. They pour water into a stone bowl and one bathes his face while the others stand apart in silence. It occurs to Lazarus that there is no sound in the sick room, or even outside, in the garden he knows so well, where birds and cicadas should be singing. The dream is also silent. He wonders if this is a condition of his death and whether he would survive if he could hear something. When the woman finishes and stands back he sees her lips moving, and he strains to listen. But there is no sound, and a few moments later he is in the other room again, watching the shadow move behind a lighted veil.

*

I am trying to remember an afternoon in summer, but the memory is too formal, and it keeps me at a distance. I see in detail the broken wall of the churchyard, the rows of pines and stones, the brilliant reds of fresh carnations and the faded pastels of silk flowers on the graves. It was a Sunday, very warm in the sun, so the shade seemed cooler and darker: I remember a faint scent on my skin and the half-fever of the heat. I have an impression of being far inland, away from the cities, in a place where nothing ever happened – as if that place were a kind of paradise, where people lived their allotted years and died of old age, half-smiling, like children exhausted by a long party, falling asleep and waking in the next parish, with new names and faces, knowing what life would bring and ready to repeat it again.

There are several possible resurrections, but the one I find easiest to imagine is the partial return of floating unseen over a garden still thick with memorised details: a return that could easily be an hallucination, where nothing is new – abandoned cups of tea and brackish water on the steps; a silent child, self-absorbed amongst the hostas and ferns; colonies of ground elder pressed to the garden wall, probing the bounds, finding cracks. I can imagine floating in the summer light, the sensation of being closer to the distance than to the house and garden below, the sensation of being pulled, as if caught in an undertow, away from the red peonies and mown grass, towards the empty pine trees in the hills, the dry slopes of sand and gorse, the cool darkness, silence.

*

When Lazarus wakes, inside the tomb, there is noise. It is not the broken sounds of the day he hears; this noise is a flow, as continuous as night. At first he thinks this river of sound is no longer happening – it is something that has remained printed on his mind like black footprints after someone has crossed wet grass – but after a while it begins to change and he knows the sounds are real: splashing cries, hushed voices, the sounds of mourning in its last stages. It is a sublittoral world beyond the stone: he finds things there he has never heard before. When the people move away they are replaced by birdsong, and he turns back to himself, to the bird-smell of his dead body, the tightness of his skin, a thread of sweetness in his throat as if he had recently swallowed honey. From time to time he sleeps, or seems to sleep. When he wakes, or seems to wake, he is waiting for something. Sometimes he has the unexpected feeling that a child is in the tomb beside him, asking questions he cannot answer: does memory reside in perfumes or sounds? are some pieces of time identical? does everything flow away or does it stand forever, perfectly still?

*

I understand that the dead are naked. They remember nothing: as soon as the graves are sealed, they begin moving away from their loves and griefs, forgetting their houses and gardens, forgetting those episodes on crowded streets, when their bodies were drenched with cold or the beating of wings, in a dizzying moment of foresight. They are walking away in a field of barley, chest-deep in warmth and undertow, feeling their bodies stray with each tug of the wind and thinking it no great loss, to begin again. It's important to admit that these named individuals disappear. We know they go into darkness, it's the only way they could ever start over. They go into darkness and whatever it is that continues goes on without them. Something they borrowed, some scrap of soul or grace, something that was never theirs alone – whatever that is, survives. Even the faithful suspect this is true. They talk about the soul, they pretend it's a personal matter but, in their hearts, they know the soul is only immortal because it belongs to no one. It keeps taking the form of an individual, but the only way it can persist is to shed that form, the way a locust sheds its skin and emerges, glistening, into the new.

*

Lazarus has become aware of something that is too large for the limited space of the tomb. He waits to recognise this presence: he wants to see, even if it is hideous, or terrifying in its beauty. He wants to give it a name. This is the constant temptation: to use the name of a god, to make it lifesize and personal, just as it is a constant temptation to see the soul as an individual belonging or property. Even though he knows these things belong to nobody, Lazarus wants to pin them down, and he is surprised when he realises the word he is searching for has slipped his mind. The harder he tries to remember, the stronger his sense of the presence becomes, until it fills the space inside the tomb, encompassing him, even while it has no form or dimension he can describe. It is perfectly dark and silent in the tomb, yet Lazarus is aware of the garden beyond the stone, the sounds of birds and running water, the perfumes and colours, the textures. He knows the presence is outside too. It is not a dogma; it is not something he chooses to believe.

Later, people come to roll away the stone. Lazarus rises and walks into the heat. When he reaches the entrance, his first act is to turn, to see what was there beside him in the dark. The tomb is empty. Or at least, nothing is visible. He expects as much and is grateful he could not remember the name of his god. When he turns back to the crowd, Jesus is standing before him. He sees no one else, only Jesus, and for a moment he understands that Jesus is more Lazarus than Lazarus has ever been. At the same time, he knows it was Jesus beside him in the tomb, keeping him awake, till the man he knows as Jesus could travel from Betharaba, beyond the Jordan, to raise him from the dead.

*

I remember being at home, then I remember being somewhere else, but I have no memory of leaving. All I know is the stories suddenly stopped. I remember the houses and the churchyard, but no people except my mother and her friends – though strangers sometimes came, in wet or dusty cars full of children and dogs, in a strange and compacted space that seemed pressed against the rear and side windows, a space they carried with them all the time, smudged with rain and motorway lights. The people came to see the church, which was partly Saxon, but they always seemed to find less than they had expected. Perhaps they had read a description in a tourist guide and assumed it would be prepared for their visit, specially cleaned, cheerful with bells and a choir.

In reality, the church was silent, and almost empty of decoration. Sometimes it was locked. When they did get in, the people found a cool, whitewashed space with an altar at one end and a plain glass window at the other. Some folded xeroxed sheets lay on a pine table by the door: a history of treasures owned and lost. The people looked, walked about, touched things, and went home disappointed. What they missed was everything the guide books omitted: bottles of greenish water in a stone coffin; a besom in the corner; a handbrush and a dustpan full of dried leaves and beetles shells; the wet, mould-stained patch on the wall where the holy spirit burrowed through in the night.

Later, if it rained, the air would close around us and we were each alone in a separate part of the house. We could not stay together. We would drift into corners and alcoves, or stumble upon one another, like strangers in the house, reading in a window seat, or behind a curtain. I would sit on the upstairs landing, looking out at the trees in the churchyard. It was as if the rest of the world had disappeared, and I was glad. I could imagine we lived on an island, surrounded by something I could almost feel on my skin, a medium the light or the wind could enter and roam in at will, sliding in to touch me then moving away again, leaving only the faintest afterprint on my skin, as if something had gripped me gently then, just as suddenly, had let go.

*

After his resurrection, Lazarus stays in the garden. It has changed, he thinks: the sound of the stream that feeds the pool is subtler, more varied, the shadows under the trees are deeper and cooler. He stays outside: even at night his sisters cannot persuade him into the house. It is not that he fears the closed space of his room: nothing reminds him of the grave, but he wants to feel space above him, the slight pressure, the special quality of being visible that he only experiences out of doors.

All day the sunlight rubs against the house like a smooth-skinned animal and the sisters feel he is somehow implicated in the heat, for how else could he sit motionless in the full sun? At night they watch him from the house. It seems he never sleeps, but he is so still, so quiet, that he might be sleeping all the time. Sometimes they think he is aware of being watched: a white, formalised being, like some lesser Egyptian god, part-cat, part-moonlight.

What he remembers now is something he has never seen. There is no sound attached to his memory; the image is one that was passed on to him by a sea-trader he had met years before: an image so hard and precise he can hold it in his mind and turn it over, like a piece of driftwood, or a pebble. The trader had spoken of a people who bred children in glass jars, using a secret mixture of seaweed and blood.

The children were born with bright green eyes and golden hair; they were treated as the favourites of the gods, living freely in the temples; then, at the age of twelve, they were sacrificed to the spirit of tides.

Lazarus does not believe this story, but he is struck by the idea that the soul is a glass, or a creature bred in glass, a beginning, a birth. What you expect to grow there, grows: a thread of blood, smears of tissue and keratin, muscle and tendons, brain, liver, heart. Tiny mouselike bones, webbed hands; veined, hairless skin stretched tight across the skull, the eyes clenched, black under the finely-wrinkled lids; the mouth toothless, sucking air. You expect it to be an imago, finally, of yourself, and you are surprised when it has a life of its own behind the veil: its own waking; its own thoughts; its own hunger.

After the resurrection, Lazarus lives a life of grace, not because he has died and been raised, but because he knows there is no secret in the grave. The only secret is the one he has refused to admit all along: the noises in the dark he hears now every night: a light metallic tapping like finger cymbals, a series of thin, dry whistles, too erratic to be intended as music, the breathing of entire armies beyond the garden wall. Other noises: a confused babble at first, but there always emerges a single convincing sound: someone is walking steadily towards him out of the darkness, moving closer and closer, someone else at first, then Lazarus himself, resuming, finding his place, ready to begin the work of forgetting.

The sisters watch. They cannot believe his body is unmarked, that it is possessed of an almost impossible cleanness, and they watch for some sign of decay: fissures in the skin, a stickiness, the first bad odour. They keep expecting him to speak, to tell them the story of his death. But Lazarus is silent. Nothing reminds him of death, but he has a partial memory of the soul or rather, not the soul, but the idea of a soul, half-pulse, half-wound, like a skylark's song-threaded larynx.

Clutter

Ziranna Zateli

GLIKERIA SAW HIM BEHIND the half-opened door. She was the young woman who brought his wife her milk every day, stopping first at his pastry store to pick up two honey cakes – 'writhing in syrup,' the way she liked them – one for her, as a thank-you, and the other one for Veta.

That morning she had found the pastry store closed. The blinds were not down, but the door was pulled shut and a large red padlock had been hooked through the door-latch. She looked at the sign which he put up when he went out for a short while: WILL BE BACK SOON.

She put the large milk pail down – she delivered to other houses too – and waited for a few minutes, fixing her hair and her bodice in the dark glass of the store. She had such beautiful fire-blond hair that she never cut it, and for years it had grown longer and longer, until it touched the small of her back. In those days people called such hair 'fateful'. She liked that: Glikeria's fateful hair. It added a new dimension to the harsh, impoverished life she spent with cows, goats, milking, and the rancid smell of whey that had seeped deep into her skin and followed her everywhere like a second shadow.

She was going to be late, and Diomedes was still nowhere to be seen. She rattled the locked door and, holding her face down to the padlock by the gap in the wood, she shouted: 'Stop playing games, Diomedes!' – not because she minded that Diomedes had not returned right away, but because she wasn't going to get her honey cakes. She took the milk and left.

She walked up the road to the left of the pastry store, turned right, passed the Arch of Tsimourta, turned left and then left again until she reached the house that belonged to Diomedes and Veta. The front door was always open. She quickly crossed the large stone courtyard – a hair had been constantly falling into her eye since the morning ('I'm going to run into someone,' she thought, and climbed the stairs).

'Is that you?' she heard in Veta's high-pitched, panting voice.

She didn't bother to answer. Veta always called out the same question whenever she heard footsteps on the stairs, always with anxiety and impatience, as if she were expecting a murderer who was late. She never called out a name, only 'Is that you? Is that you?' She could quickly say it five times over.

'How can Veta put up with such a life?' Glikeria thought in spite of herself. 'What's the point?'

She found her, as always, stretched out, paralyzed, on the floor. Every morning that was how Veta wanted Diomedes to lay her out before he went to the store. And she lay there – managing with the utmost effort to tug her skeletal, nearly dead body a few inches – until evening, when Diomedes would put her back to bed, wiping her body of filth, washing her face, her armpits, her legs, and feeding her. At lunchtime he would come for half an hour. He would feed her on the floor. The rest of his time he spent either in the pastry store, inventing elaborate, unheard-of pastries – the honey cakes Glikeria chose were his simplest creations – or reading detective novels. Of his great misfortune when twelve years ago, a few months after his marriage, the gradual and unrelenting paralysis of his wife had set in, he spoke to no one. He had taken her to many doctors, even in Europe. There was no hope for a cure – except death. He sank into deep, silent acceptance of his destiny, and immersed himself in the creation of the most exquisite pastry that enchanted everyone, so from that standpoint things were going brilliantly.

The door to Veta's room was open, as were the two windows. It was summer, and in an hour or two the heat would become unbearable. Veta's large shining eyes, black like olives, and so benevolent and wild, again took Glikeria by surprise, although she saw them every morning.

'Veta, why don't you sleep until I come? Why don't you close your eyes for a bit?' she almost scolded her.

The paralyzed woman laughed – a chimpanzee laugh, Glikeria thought – she was definitely trying to express something with that laugh, but neither she, nor certainly Glikeria, knew what.

'There are no honey cakes today, Veta. Diomedes wasn't in the store,' she told her. 'You'll have to drink your milk plain, like a good girl.'

And she went into the kitchen, poured the alloted amount of milk into a pot, and from it filled a small coffee pot with milk and put it on the gas to boil so she could give it to the sick woman – Diomedes also paid her to do this.

Veta was saying something in the other room, something about Diomedes, Glikeria thought, but her mouth, which had been hanging open for twelve years now, the lower lip completely twisted, had again become besotted with spittle, and Glikeria could not understand a thing.

She spat into her palm the seeds of three dates she had found on a plate in the kitchen and stuffed into her mouth, went back to Veta's room, and with a large piece of cloth wiped away the spittle that was seeping out of the paralyzed woman's mouth. More spit gushed out, in greater volume, as if gently and freely she were spewing up opaque, bubbly water.

'Wait a minute, keep quiet,' Glikeria told her. 'I'm just going to get the milk before it boils over.' And she ran back into the kitchen.

She stuffed two more dates into her mouth – 'You thieving glutton,' she murmured to herself as the sweet exotic fruit melted on her tongue; their cost kept her from having them in her own house. She dropped three more into her pocket, and then with her fingers scattered about the few that were left on the plate so that it wouldn't be too obvious that she had swiped some, although she was sure that Diomedes wouldn't say anything the next day. But she was ashamed of her greed.

And then she saw right opposite her, behind the half-open door to the right of Veta's room – she saw the crease in his black pants; saw the black, well-polished shoe; she even noticed the delicate plastic edges of his black shoelaces, and the delicate stripes of his sock... and Glikeria noticed an infinite number of other details as the milk by her side frothed up, boiled over, and spattered on the gas stove, an infinite number of details... as long as she didn't have to acknowledge, to admit, to conceive what she saw before her: a leg hanging in the air. In the air.

Veta's voice in the other room was coming through now like the howl of a dog, and Glikeria, hypnotized by the horror that was frantically trying to express itself, walked towards the half-opened door, and pushed it. It resisted slightly, she pushed it harder, her body was growing numb, was becoming empty, the door overcame the ghastly obstacle, hit the wall and stayed wide open... Diomedes' long body inside his black wedding suit rolled and pitched towards her icy eyes and swung away from her in the air... And then she remembered the sign on the other door, WILL BE BACK SOON. She saw his tongue which stuck out to mock her. Almost tenderly, completely incapable of taking in the deed, she whispered: 'Stop playing games, Diomedes.'

She left Veta whimpering, and then when she bolted down the stairs, howling like a dog. She rushed out into the courtyard and lunging into the street she seized her long, fateful hair, and with a single passionate, maniacal movement wrenched it apart and hurled the two strands at her face again and again. She wanted to speak, to scream, to say what she had seen, but she couldn't, and she whipped herself over and over with the strands of hair that were like the tails of wild horses that would bring back her speech.

*

The neighbors who began climbing the stairs – Veta was now almost bursting her near-useless vocal cords constantly shouting 'Is that you? Is that you?' found the house reeking of seared milk and gas, even though the windows were open. The paralyzed woman's eyes were crazed, and there was a large puddle of her saliva on the floor. She wanted her milk, but had forgotten how to ask for it in a human voice, and was begging with an animal's howls.

*

They took Diomedes down. According to a relative of his who was a lawyer, he had hung himself in 'a near-perfect and quite original manner'. He must have been preparing the setup, the tools, the conditions for at least two or three days. And he had obviously been convinced that he would not fail. He had hung himself right behind the door at the point where it opened. He didn't need to kick away a chair or stool; having tied the rope tightly around his neck, all he had to do was grab the door and forcefully, with a steady hand, slam it shut. He knew the door wouldn't close completely, but he had provided for that too, so that that would not be essential for hoisting his body in the air within a fraction of a second, his neck securely trapped in the noose.

He had devised a super-logical, paranoiac pulley system above the door by connecting it to the ceiling, thus creating 'an unheard-of but surefire system for committing suicide', according again to his lawyer relative, and to the general consensus of those who untied him, and even of those who just saw the setup and ran their trembling fingers over the pulleys, and finally those who were brought in to dismantle it.

On his bed, on the other side of the room, he had left a letter written minutes before his final deed, asking that they not abuse his body (in parentheses he had written that he had bathed himself and, as everyone could see, dressed himself as befitted the occasion). He asked that they bury him as quickly as possible, in other words on the same day. He begged his aunt to feed his wife at noon and in the evening (again in parentheses, he had written that he himself had cooked her food, chicken broth with bits of tiny pasta and vitamins in it, early that morning). His final request was that they open the pastry store (the key was under the stone to the left of the door) and let the children go on a rampage through it. He bade them farewell and signed his name.

In a postscript on a separate sheet of paper he noted that he was not leaving behind any debts, a needless statement as everyone was aware of his almost pathological aversion to debts of any kind: he had even paid Glikeria, with the sum rounded off, on the first of every month for the following month, not, like everyone else, for the month that had passed.

*

That day Veta struggled in vain to tell people that she had heard something, a strange sound in the next room that had frightened her, just before Glikeria had brought her her milk.

Diomedes had gotten up at five this morning, maybe even earlier. He drank his coffee in the kitchen and cooked chicken soup for Veta – later he told her: 'I might be busy at lunch; I cooked the food and put in the vitamins; I'll send Aunt Marika over to feed you – you must eat all your soup, like a good girl.' She heard him take a bath, then he lifted her out of bed and went to the store. She didn't hear him return home, nor did she see him pass her room to go to his. But there was a second door to his room with stairs going down to the back of the house.

Veta had heard a sound at some point and had become frightened. That is what she was struggling to tell them – that is what she had been struggling to tell Glikeria when Glikeria had gone into the kitchen for the milk that morning – but she couldn't bring out the words. Only disjointed sounds drowned in waves of spittle came out of her mouth, while her distraught eyes widened.

Aunt Marika fed her at lunch time, and Veta ate everything because her husband had asked her to. After the funeral, that same afternoon, his aunt came back again to feed Veta, full of anxiety as to who would care for the paralyzed woman now that Diomedes was gone. She stopped feeding her halfway through and went into the sitting room, where all the other relatives and neighbors had gathered.

'Diomedes left all his affairs in good order,' she said, moving her hand emphatically. 'But this time he left an unpaid debt, a living debt (and with the same hand she pointed to Veta's room), and now let us see who is going to take care of this debt.' For Veta had neither parents nor brothers and sisters – she had no relatives of her own.

As she returned to Veta's room, Aunt Marika found Glikeria feeding the paralyzed woman.

'*I'm* going to feed her from now on!' Glikeria said emphatically. 'You should be ashamed of yourself, you his aunt, to speak this way in his house!' and a terrible fight followed on which it would be better for us not to dwell.

In the next room the lawyer was emptying out a trunk full of Diomedes' books – paperback detective novels – and was piling them into cardboard boxes. He had found another large batch in the cellar of the pastry store, and he took those as well.

'I wonder how much time I'll need,' he was saying to himself, 'to read all of them? Three months? Six months? A year? Two years? I'm going to read them all! Somewhere inside this clutter of second rate mystery novels I'll find the dark idea that inspired him. The dark idea, the darkest idea he ever had in his life.'

That evening came the first signs that Veta's paralysis would become complete very soon. If she could still drag herself a few inches along the floor, soon she would be completely confined to her bed, staring up at the ceiling until she expired.

And that came about much faster than anyone expected. The following day, around noon, without having moved from her bed, without asking to be put down on the floor, without inarticulate calls and without moving her eyes from the ceiling or closing them, Veta expired. Five or six relatives were in the room talking, and at least twenty minutes passed before anyone noticed, by which time her extremities had gone cold and her nose had become discolored.

Everyone regarded it as a mysterious, miraculous act of nature. There was no reason for an autopsy. She was buried next to Diomedes.

*

After many months of reading, the tenacious lawyer felt that he had found in that 'clutter of second-rate mystery novels' the scheme that had inspired Diomedes to stage his departure from his life of agony at the exact moment of his choice.

It was a story, one could say a touchingly mediocre one, by an unknown English writer who did not have any particular expectations from his muse – but that is not to say that he wasn't adept at setting up and developing the plot of a basic mystery novel – obviously each time with different motives, settings, and characters.

The protagonist of the book is a middle-aged aristocrat who is madly in love with his exceptionally beautiful young wife. Having to choose between an honorable death (suicide), or be subjected to the shame and humiliation of the gradual disclosure of a smuggling ring of which he is the leader, he chooses the first option. Setting out to prepare himself carefully for the deed, he strives not only to insure its success, but also to procure people's admiration for the 'technique' of his suicide. He is found hanging behind his office door, in a perfect manner...

The following day his wife dies too. The autopsy uncovers traces of poison. There are many suspects, except, of course, her dead husband.

But thanks to the intuition and persistence of an amateur detective, who is related to the hero and who pledges to learn the secret for his own peace of mind, the dead husband is revealed as his wife's murderer. The detective is instinctively drawn to the books, papers, and documents that had been the dead man's obsession, and finds that for days he had systematically poisoned his wife by pouring a carefully calculated dose of poison into the elegant bottle of a rare liqueur that only she drank – two glasses every evening. This particular poison had no visible results or side effects whatsoever, except for an occasional innocent dizzy spell, until the required amount had been accumulated in daily dosages. According to the murderer's calculations, his wife would die forty-eight hours after he did, as she remained faithful to her invariable two nightly glasses of liqueur.

His wife emptied the ornate bottle even earlier.

The reason he wished for her death was his morbid jealousy, his inability to envision her in the arms of another man.

*

Diomedes' relative did not speak to anyone about what he had found in this tattered paperback. After all, Diomedes had a much more serious reason to wish for his wife's death – that is, if it wasn't his wife's tragic condition that had actually driven him to suicide.

The smuggler-aristocrat's relative, the amateur detective in the book, also did not reveal – for other reasons – the truth which he in his turn had found in an old silver-bound book containing a similar tale of another era.

Translated from the Greek
Peter Constantine

Kalsang's Brother

Regi Claire

MISS ROBINSON is four foot ten, with sharp lime-green eyes and a voice like a metal spoon scraping out one of her saucepans. No matter how loud the hiss of frying fat or water boiling over, she can always make herself heard. Nothing escapes her notice: two sprinklings of pepper instead of one, and her girls are in for a lecture on the effects of 'too much spice'.

Not that Miss Robinson's had a taste of the *real* spice of life so far; that, unfortunately, has never yet come her way. Still, there's nothing obviously wrong with her: she looks sturdy enough, her hair is a natural pale yellow, the kind that doesn't grey easily, and when she smiles, which is not too often and more like a glare, her teeth are unexpectedly white and even.

In her heart of hearts she longs for someone to sweep her off the painstakingly polished floor-tiles of the domestic science kitchen and carry her away, but as soon as she finds herself in company, whether male or female, she feels so terribly, terribly small that her tone invariably grows shrill and virginally abrasive. Sometimes in class, before allowing the girls to sit down to their jointly produced meals, she stares at them and announces, scouring-strength, how she doesn't want them to gorge themselves and that they must learn to stop at the point where they can still force down a slice of stale bread.

*

It's Wednesday, 10.17 am by the staff-room clock. Miss Robinson is bracing herself for another show-down with the new bunch of thirteen-year-olds she was assigned a few weeks ago, in mid-term. By the time she rinses out her cup her breath has a bitter flare to it that's not entirely due to the coffee.

The door of her classroom is closed, but the girls inside are quite definitely *not* copying down the recipes written up on the board for their lesson. They're talking. Talking in shrieks and giggles, and Miss Robinson has no difficulty picturing them lolling around the tables that double as desks, shaking their hair out over the clean formica surfaces, filing and polishing nails, and nonchalantly flicking off dead bits of skin. She herself is very neat and tidy and would never have thought of making her *toilette* anywhere except a bathroom, and then only bent over the wash-hand basin.

She grits her teeth, about to press down the doorhandle, when she hears one of the girls say 'Kalsang's brother' in a loud, excited-sounding voice. Miss Robinson hesitates. She has recognised the speaker and is appalled by the intensity of her enthusiasm. Surely, whether Kalsang has a brother or not would seem the least of Edith's worries – thin and bony Edith, who'd do much better to spend her surplus energy on eating up her food for a change. But Miss Robinson's curiosity has been whetted. Kalsang, after all, is the most unsettling creature she's come across in the nineteen years of her teaching career. Descended from Tibetan refugees who founded a colony in one of the neighbouring villages, this particular thirteen-year-old has grown up hard and sinuous and inscrutably superior, just like her name. So now there is a brother, too... If nothing else, it's Miss Robinson's duty to find out more. Stooping slightly, she leans forward –

'Oh, hello Miss. Sorry we're late. There were queues at the check-outs.'

Miss Robinson spins round, draws herself up with a gasp and darts furious glances at the three girls who've caught her lingering beside her own door, five minutes after the bell has rung. Sonja and Angela, the two Italians, are holding up their carrier bags on angled arms, awkwardly, like shields; Kalsang stands behind them, eyes gleaming in the wooden darkness of her face, waiting, and very, very tall. For several seconds nobody speaks. Then Miss Robinson reaches out for their shopping:

'Well, at last. I hope you haven't forgotten anything.'

*

The classroom is on two levels. There's a small entrance hall on the ground floor, its furnishings an umbrella stand and two rows of coat hooks Miss Robinson has all to herself, plus a bulb set into the ceiling like a solitary eye. A vicious, nostril-pinching smell comes from an adjacent boxroom which is crammed with detergents, floor cloths, mops, buckets and brushes, a square old porcelain sink, chipped and lustreless after too many scrubbings, and – squat behind a shower curtain – a toilet. A sign above it says, FOR SLOPS ONLY, 'slops' being underlined twice.

A short flight of steps leads up to the mezzanine, where the cookery room proper mirrors itself in a window-front that runs the length of the far wall and gives on to the school yard. The four custom-built kitchen areas, all equally sparkling, enclose a space in the centre for tables, chairs and a blackboard on wheels.

When Miss Robinson enters, hidden behind the three latecomers because she's felt it necessary to check through their purchases first, the blackboard's been moved and is just wheezing to a halt near the steps, swinging loosely in its frame like a giant's nodding head. Peals of laughter ring out before she has a chance to see what's been going on: underneath the recipes on the board someone's chalked a puckered-up potato face.

'Watch it, girls, or you'll be staying in again,' Miss Robinson says scratchily and to no-one in particular, trying to keep her temper, for the moment at least. Then she points with one of the shopping bags: 'Edith, please, would you mind wiping this off? And put the board back in its right position – if you can manage, that is.' She hasn't meant to say the last few words aloud, hasn't meant to be hurtful, but Edith's unnatural thinness annoys her; it's a waste and an affront, an obscenity really, made all the more poignant by the loose-fitting muslin dress that keeps drooping and caving in on the girl. And *her* talking about boys!

Disgusted, Miss Robinson turns away. She ignores the twitter around her, yet, crossing over to the fridge, becomes aware of walking lopsidedly, as though a piece of mud had got stuck in the tread of her left shoe. Of course she knows it's nothing, the floor's as clean as a new pin, just her imagination playing up again. So she stamps her foot hard twice, and that seems to do the trick. There's silence afterwards. But the class hasn't been taken in by her manoeuvre – they're simply biding their time.

*

The first period is nutrition theory. As usual, Miss Robinson sits perched on her swivel chair opposite her pupils. They remind her of cut-outs pasted on glass, especially now, with the late-morning sun pushing in through the line of windows into the room behind them. Pushing in mercilessly. Already, the trees outside have a dark, skewered look and their shadows appear stunted out of all proportion.

Before beginning the lesson, Miss Robinson had swept across the yard with a long, harsh stare that seemed to swirl the litter on the ground into a heap out of sight and to bodily lift and straighten up the few schoolchildren who happened to be slouching about. Only the Tinguely Metal Man, towering ten feet high in his concrete-slabbed fountain, has remained as he was. Perfectly indifferent to light and shadow and to how or whether they affect his size, he continues balancing his cannon ball, letting it rumble from claw-like hand to claw-like hand, with the easy reassurance of someone who knows how to hold their own. Miss Robinson's gaze keeps returning to him. He's helped her through lessons before.

'So,' Miss Robinson grates, her eyes flitting from table to table, from face to face, 'what are the main constituents of food, then?' She's nicknamed the three sets of girls that make up the cooking teams 'sex', 'meat', and 'brains' – a private joke to jog her memory.

'Chocolate,' Myrtle cries, winking at the others as she smacks her lips rather unashamedly (she is a member of team one, has a sallow face and a sluggish, full-blown body that strains the seams of her dresses).

Miss Robinson merely purses her mouth: 'Anyone?'

Sonja, elbow on table, raises a forefinger: 'Protein, carbohydrate, fat.'

Sadly enough, it's the girls of foreign background who are the most promising in this class, Miss Robinson muses as she gives a brisk nod. The local stock is represented either by cuddly little pussy cats à la Myrtle & Co., groomed and licked and slicked into shape, or a more degenerate strain preoccupied with food (it's impossible not to swivel round towards Edith, half-dead after her little task, and her two friends, Gaby the guzzler, and Kate with her equine features and puritan abhorrence of flesh). Miss Robinson feels an itch of annoyance spreading down her legs.

'Anything else you can think of? Kalsang?' She looks over at the girl, then away again, but not quickly enough. Because for that one second *there*'s Kalsang's brother, his image reflected in his sister's face, his eyes as black and lidless as hers, only more slanted, the cheekbones even higher, bronzier, the lips thin, chiselled almost, though without that disdainful curve ('defiant' might have been an apter description, but Miss Robinson doesn't always choose her words wisely).

'Well?' Miss Robinson tosses her head to shake off the image. A wispy giggle hangs in the air. Her itch is becoming unbearable. She jumps up and begins pacing the room, careful to avoid the advancing shafts of sunlight. The girls are watching her. Miss Robinson never walks, she marches. Like a pair of scissors slamming open and shut. Perhaps she hopes to intimidate them or to make up for the flat-heeled children's shoes she's forced to wear because her feet are too small to fit adult sizes. Now, all at once, she shouts, 'Pull those blinds down, someone! And get out your books!'

*

It's after eleven, and Miss Robinson has brought herself back under control. She is demonstrating how to prepare the various dishes on today's menu, pretending not to be bothered by the girls' shoulders blocking her view.

'Next comes the ruler,' she says, perhaps a trifle shrilly, and slaps the pink plastic onto the rolled-out puff pastry in front of her, measures, then cuts it with a knife: 'Five-inch squares... like this... should give you twelve croissants, OK?' Standing on tiptoe for a moment she raises her voice: 'Now for the ham filling – two spoonfuls a square, that's what the recipe's calculated for, no more, no less. Anyway, you don't want to gorge yourselves. Better to...'

None of the girls are listening, they've heard it all before. Behind Miss Robinson's back, Gaby's telling Edith not to worry, she'll help her dispose of things no problem – and Kate's share of ham into the bargain. Kate smiles her horsey smile while Edith starts nudging Kalsang, who's staring past Miss Robinson's impeccably bobbed hair at the thick fabric of the blinds, her mouth sneering softly. Kalsang's in one of her dazes, has her brother on her mind no doubt.

Suddenly Miss Robinson swings round, her eyes fizzy with suspicion. It's a habit of hers, and it does pay off occasionally: this time she's caught Myrtle's hand in the act as it were, picking stray hairs off her best friend's blouse and dropping them casually on the floor, long ropey hairs that coil nastily on the shiny tiles, clearly visible.

'Myrtle, you'll be doing the mopping today.' Miss Robinson's voice dips and dangles dangerously, like a fork ready to pierce. She knows she mustn't lose her grip again and strains every nerve to imagine the Metal Man in his corner, *her* Metal Man – so strong, so utterly imperturbable.

*

This Wednesday Miss Robinson is eating with Kalsang, Sonja and Angela. She does her best to engage them in conversation, praising the salad dressing, then the artistic shape of their croissants, then re-introducing the topic of proteins, carbohydrates, fats, vitamins and minerals from the most playful angle she can think of:

'They're a bit like friends,' she says with a laugh that bares her teeth, 'or acquaintances, enemies even – to be sought out, ignored or best avoided!'

But the three girls remain silent. They don't like Miss Robinson. Somehow, she always makes them feel as though they're guests who haven't been invited. She seems to act the part of host – and act it very badly: there's no grace in her performance, no warmth or generosity, only restraint and a tedious obsession with detail. Just like when she tells them to wash up the floor around their kitchen area the instant something gets spilt ('In case you tread in it and smear it all over the classroom'); or when she keeps them in till they've steel-woolled away half their hotplates and vinegar-shined the chromium of their sink and draining-board so insanely it could have been mistaken for an extra-large mirror in a beauty parlour.

Halfway through the meal there's a tap at the window in the far corner. It's too faint to be remarkable really, a bee perhaps, hoping to get at the nectar inside the bright red of the blind, or an empty snack packet being blown about – except, of course, that the bees are late this year, and the day windless, as calm and unmoved as the Metal Man's face. Whatever the reason, Miss Robinson, for once, is blissfully unaware, having just bitten into another croissant. But the girls glance at each other and their eyes flicker. Afterwards they talk more loudly and laugh a lot, in a childish, blurting, vulgar way that makes Miss Robinson shrink inside.

Dessert over ('A touch sugary, your *compote*, Angela. Remember that men, especially husbands, don't like things too sweet'), she pushes back her chair with a screech. This is the time when she stands her straightest, her hands lifted for a moment as if to steady an imaginary ball. 'Kalsang, you too! We're in a Christian country here!' Miss Robinson wants the girls to be grateful for the food they cook, that's all. Ready to have to glare them into submission she is surprised to find there's no problem today: all heads are bent, meek and attentive. 'Mary had a little lamb,' goes through her mind and, folding her hands, she congratulates herself on her teaching skills, then begins:

'For that which we have just eaten may –'

Something has clattered against the windows outside, a whole volley of small stones or nails that will leave the surface pitted with tiny sharp craters no amount of polishing can erase. Miss Robinson is off like a shot, she feels personally attacked, defiled even: to be interrupted in the middle of a prayer!

The girls' lips twitch as they watch her yank up the nearest blind. They know she won't see a soul out there at first, only the dirty emptiness of the yard. They know that as soon as she's flung open the sash to lean forward a group of boys in outsize T-shirts, back-to-front caps and daringly low-slung jeans will come skateboarding into view, gliding past her in single file; and that she'll start yelling at each of them in turn, most likely making futile threats involving the headmaster. And the girls also know that the boys will ignore the shouts and put on a show specially for her, blowing kisses.

*

Abruptly Miss Robinson jerks away from the window; there was a noise behind her from the boxroom, she's quite sure – the boxroom that should have been *empty*.

'Who's there?' she calls out. No-one replies, not a sound. She eyes her class sharply; none of them are missing, none of them move. None of them look at her. Kalsang appears to be shuttered in a silent wild world of her own, like a woodcut under glass.

'Answer me!' Miss Robinson rushes towards the steps leading down to the entrance hall, then stops short to listen. Someone's in that room, she's certain, messing about with her cloths and cleaners, her buckets, her mops. Didn't she hear a noise, distinctly hear it, a minute ago? She twists back towards the girls; it's obvious to her they're merely pretending not to have noticed, holding their breath all the while.

Miss Robinson is getting very upset. Already she is too upset to focus on her Metal Man. And when she tries to picture Kalsang's brother instead, when she tries and tries and tries, there's nothing but a blank in his place and even Kalsang's face begins to look blurred now.

The only thing Miss Robinson can see clearly as she turns away from her class at last is her own shadow, lengthening towards sunset.

The Resurrection o Lazarus

from Dario Fo's Mistero Buffo

HEY! WID THIS be the kirkyaird whaur there's tae be the resurrection o Lazarus?

Aye, this is it.

That's fine than.

Bide a wee – saxpence tae come by.

Saxpence?

Thripence than.

Thripence – whit for?

Becus it's me that luiks aifter this kirkyaird an ye fowk come breengin in ramstam an spile the hedges an traimple doon the girss anna an I maun hae a wee bit for aa the baither an aa the wark ye gar me pit up wi. Thripence or ye dinna see the miracle.

Ah weel, ye're a richt fly ane.

Thripence ye tae and I dinna care if ye hae bairns wi ye – it's aa the same tae me – they can keek as weel, no? Richt than – a bawbee. Get affen that wa, ye muckle ideeot. He'd like fine tae see the miracle fir nocht. Are ye gaun tae pey or no? Thripence – no, ye didna pey. Thripence, ye anes – thripence tae come by.

He's recht shairp, that yin. He maks a bonny penny wi the miracles. Noo A maun see whaur this Lazarus is. There maun be his name abune the tomb anna. That ither time A cam here tae see the miracle wrocht A wis here a'most hauf the day jist wyting an than they gaed an hid the miracle doun by. There A wis staunin like a gowk. But this time like A ken the name. A fand it oot. A'll find the name on the stane. A'll be the first like. A'll staun richt there afore the tomb an A'll see aathing frae the beginnin like. That's it – bit even if A sud find the stane wi Lazarus on it A cannae read. Ah weel! A'll jist guess. A'll staun richt here. That ither time it was nae guid – maybe it'll be better this time. Hey dinna ye try tae push me! A wis here afore ye an A'm gauna staun at the front. A dinna care if ye're a wee bit thing. The wee yins sud come early in the mornin tae find a place. Stan in a row, the ane ahint the ither wi the wee yins in front an the big yins ahint. Aye an than the wee yins can come late an micht as weel hae come early! Dinna push – ye'll gar me fa right intae the grave. Tae hell, man, it's naething tae do wi me. Ye're at the back! Eh? So it's the wimmen that's pushin neist!

Is he no comin? Isna it time fir the miracle?

Is there naebody that kens this Jesus Christ an cud mibbe rin an tell him that we're aa here ready an wytin? We canna bide here a day wytin for the miracle, cin we?

There sud be a time gien oot fir sic-like things.

Chears! wha needs a chear? Ladies, tak a chear! Thripence a chear. Taka chear an sit yerselves doon becus whan there's the miracle an the haily man gars Lazarus come oot on his twa feet, talkin, singin, movin, it'll gie ye sic a fleg whan there's a glint in his een that ye'll cowp ower backlins an gie yer heids sic a dunt on a stane that' ye'll be deid, Deid! An the haly man doesnae dae mair than the wan miracle a day. Tak a chear! Thripence.

That's aa he thinks about – the pennies.

Sae naebody'll ging –

Dinna push – I dinna care!

Dinna staun on the chears – he's no blate though. Did ye see that wee yin – he's staunin on the chear.

Is he comin? No – he isna.

Chips! a penny the poke. Chips that guid they'd bring the deid tae lifel A penny the poke.

Gie Lazarus a poke tae start aff wi.

Haud yer wheesht, blasphemer.

Het chips.

He's comin. He's comin. He's here.

Whitna ane is he?

Jesus!

Whit ane?

The wan wi the black face? I dinna like the wey he glowers.

No, no. that yin's Mark.

The yin ahint?

The big yin?

No, the wee yin.

The hauflin?

The ain wi the beard anna.

He luiks like a hauflin tae me, dammit if he disnae.

Luk! they're aa there!

Hey, John! A ken him – John, John. A real nice face, Jesus.

Luik! there's the Madonna as weel. There's aa his kith an kin. He's aye got them wi him.

They dinna lat him oot an aboot alane – he's no richt i the heid.

Jesus! Oh A like that yin. He gied me a wink anna.

Jesus, Jesus, dae the miracle wi the loaves an the fishes like that ither time whan they were that guid.

Haud yer wheesht, blasphemer. Behave yersel.

Wheesht, doun on yer knees. He's tauld us tae get doon on our knees. We maun pray.

No, I'll no get doon on ma knees – I dinna haud wi that. Whaur's the tomb?

Eh? – it's that ane doun there.

Oh luik – he's tellt them tae tak aff the muckle stane. That's great.

Wheesht!

Lat me see!

No, get affen that chear!

Lat me up, A need tae see!

Jesus, luik, They've taen up the muckle stane. There's the deid man. He's in there anna – it's Lazarus stinkin. Feech! what's that awfie stink.

Christ!

Whit's wrang?

Wheesht!

Lat me see!

He's fou o worms – o creepie-crawlies. Feech! he maun hae been deid a month – he's aa fa'in apairt. That's a fine like thing they've dune tae him. Tae Jesus. It's nae joke. I fear he'll no manage it this time, puir thing.

A'm shuir he'll no manage it. He canna dae it! There's nae wey he can mak him come oot. He's stinkin rotten. That's a fine like thing – tellin him he wasna deid mair than three days! It's a month or mair. A fine like thing. Puir Jeus!

I say he'll dae it aa the same – that yin's a haily man at cin dae the miracle even if they've been stinkin fur a month an a hauf.

An I say he canna!

Will ye wager?

I'll wager anna!

Richt than! Saxpence! A shill!n! Whitever ye like.

I'll haud it. Dae ye trust me? He dis. We aa trust each ither. Fine than – I'll tak the money.

Richt than – tak tent though. Doon on yer knees, aa body.

Whit's he daein.

He's there prayin.

Wheesht will ye!

Hey there, Lazarus, git up noo.

Oh, he cin haud forth an he cin sing if he likes – aa that'll come oot is the worms he's fu o.

Git up, I bid ye!
Wheesht, he's up on his knees.
Wha? Jesus?
No! Lazarus. God, luik at that.
Get awa wi ye – it's nae possible.
Lat me see.
Luik, luik – he's waukin, he's fa'en doon. He's staunin. On his twa feet!
A meeracle – Oh it's a meeracle. Oh Jesus, ye're a gret yin an I didna believe.
Weel dune, Jesus.
I hae won the wager. Gie's the money. Dinna try ony tricks wi me!
Weel dune, Jesus!
My purse – they've stawn ma purse. Thief!
Weel dune, Jesus!
Thief!
Weel dune Jesus! Weel dune! Thief!...

translated by Stuart Hood

COUNTERPOINTS

GERRIE FELLOWS

CORAL HULL

Counterpoints

Gerrie Fellows

HE PREACHES as they pass (Jesus will save them) but they turn away, seeing themselves dissolve in the windows (He will heal them) among pots of indigo and scented oils (He is their salvation). Among pouches of velvet with metal jaws, among high fast heels: here's how (they are absolved) they walk out, spring coming. Or sheathed in waterfall silk, their faces shining given back to them in ticking, jewelled faces of African gold. And above them all the global signs WELCOME TO AUCKLAND. Each building a trumpet blast to THE CAPITAL OF THE SOUTH PACIFIC, a jigsaw puzzle of past and future; the Victorians' ponderous curlicues impaled on the geometry of illusion.

The faces of the young distorted in windows, in ranked shields. The visors of riot police reflecting glass, high flying cloud. And under the visors the unreflective faces, the drawn down mouths, the puritanical armies of Godzone. SCHOOL'S OUT. December 1984.

Faces, bodies jostling under the banners. UNEMPLOYED WORKERS ASSOCIATION, P & T ASSOCIATION, UNEMPLOYED WORKERS MOVEMENT. April 1932. *A man will succeed here if he has probity and application.* The women sang the Red Flag. *A man has no need of association in this country of natural abundance.* The reflections shattered became splinters, jagged bracelets of glass through which to grab for cigarettes, whisky, diamonds, fallen gold. A man lined his pockets with ticking clocks, youths in dress jackets strutted on a dangerous catwalk, the police surged down Queen Street in a brutal wave.

At Tennyson Street Mrs Graham came hammering on the kitchen door to Alice and the boys, telling the news from the wireless. Riot, its flames like wildfire. And the Union meeting in the town hall, Charlie'd be stuck in there.

Charlie Fellows, my grandfather, was a telegraph linesman, a trade union activist. His father and grandfather were master-bricklayers; big chinned, stocky, handsome people with careful hands. His grandfather had come out to New Zealand in the 1880s. *For here a man must be the architect of his own fortunes.* He bought a section in Onehunga and the family lived under tarpaulin there while they built a brick house for themselves. There was work for builders. Auckland was spreading out over the Maori farms, over the peach groves and fields of maize.

> *For the Lord thy God bringeth thee into a good land, a land of brooks of water, of fountains and depths that spring out of valleys and hills; A land of wheat, and barley, and vines, and fig trees, and pomegranates; a land of oil, olive and honey; A land wherein thou shalt eat bread without scarceness, thou shalt not lack any thing in it.*

I'm standing in the museum gazing at a grainy black and white photograph of a Maori family lined up in shapeless European clothes in front of a ramshackle whare. Loss is written across their faces, into their hands, into the grey seams of their garments. It is 1928 and they are lined up to be shot by a white photographer as a record of a dying race.

In 1928 my father was seven years old doing sums at a desk in a school in Northcote. Across the water in Manukau a child was being beaten for speaking her own language. And deep in the volcanic heart of the island a man was carving a door lintel out of the living wood of his people.

Imagine, in that same year in front of the brick house in Onehunga, the Fellows family lined up together for the camera. They would all beam happily out at the photographer. There's Grandfather Fellows with the bushy moustache, and that's Ernie, he was a master bricklayer too, and Eric, and Eileen, Jean's mother, who married George Sweet, and Auntie Dot, huge woman, and Esma who married John Thomson. She had 17 kids. And that's Leslie, he was the youngest of the brothers. A celebration, Christmas, a wedding maybe. They would smile for camera, the women shading their eyes with their hats, the men a little too warm in their best suits but content, with the holiday, with their country, with the language in which they tell jokes to one another and stories to the children.

Family photographs: the Fellows brothers as young men, jaunty-chinned; Charlie with Alice Fitzgerald on their wedding day in 1919; Alice in 1926 with my father and uncle on the Sydney harbour ferry on her first visit back.

In 1917 when my grandmother crossed the Tasman loss was a secret coin she had carried with her, something durable, shining, lucky. Only years later her sons would say, I think there was someone, in Sydney, before the war. Her sisters, Dear Flo, Ada, Berthe, Maggie, she consigned to letters. She put her family at a distance, that was the story. She turned her face to the new life, got a job at the City Treasury, married a man faithful to principles and people, younger than she was, proud of her. Is that the story? In Northcote during the pinched years of the thirties she bought the stock for the co-operative and did the books. When Charlie retired they bought a shop. GIs flocked in to buy newspapers and magazines. She was a clever woman. My mother would say, bossy like her eldest son. And why did she marry a man so much younger than she was? Charlie was such a darling.

Northcote now is a place you pass. The motorway straddles Tennyson Street, Sulphur Beach, my father's childhood. The bus skims by on its way north. Auckland unwalkable: long straps of flyovers, sheets of water. The present swallows us.

By the time we knew her, ageing, irascible, not given to cuddles, she was Granny Fellows, a black-dressed territorial woman with wasp stings at her kitchen door. She and my uncle had moved south by then to a house under the cone of Mangere pa. Salt spray burnt the vegetables in the market gardens and blasted the edge of the kumara pits high on the crater of Mangere hill, but on the kitchen wall Loo's calendar bloomed with flowers and fruit, the sun shone and we drove out to Auntie Tillie in Waiuku.

*

This land and harbour of Manukau   is a ring of sacred places.
This land and harbour of Manukau   is a ring of despoilations.

From Mangere to the Waikato River: 58,475 hectares of confiscated land.

The mudflats taken for the airport, the sewage treatment plant, the LPG wharf terminal.

The shellfisheries unpredictable, dwindling, despoiled.

The body of water enriched, sickened, polluted.

The oyster shells empty
but the fishshop window glittering with oysters.

Manukau was their garden of the sea,
life sustaining body of water

enriched, sickened, polluted.

We drive south from Mangere around the rim of the Manukau, Donna at the wheel telling of other places – her father's people from Lewis, the snapshots from Carloway filled with ageing faces.

There, my uncle points out a sagging field, a gulch of tumbled pasture, a shed about to topple, that's where Eric and Tillie's farm was. (Ah, my father remembers, the summers at Maioro, the marram grass, the sand hills, the long luminous trek to the sea.) During the depression when the Post Office started cutting wages Eric got out and went farming. The Thomsons farmed here too. That was their place up the hill there, better land, not as heavy as the flat.

From Mangere to the Waikato River 58,475 hectares of confiscated land.

In the thirties there was a relief camp opposite Eric's farm, government work for the unemployed planting trees to stabilize the dunes.

1,490 hectares compulsorily purchased from the Waikato tribes for the planting of the Waiuku State Forest.

Conifers on the skyline, pyramids of black sand.

Maioro, the ancient burying ground desecrated, mined for ironsands.

DANGER KEEP OUT

The burying ground once ringed with ancestors,
their dangerous and sacred faces of carved wood.

DANGER KEEP OUT

HIGH PRESSURE SLURRY PIPELINE

THE WORLD'S FIRST POLYURETHANE-LINED HIGH PRESSURE UNDERGROUND PIPELINE TRANSPORTING ABRASIVE GRANULAR MATERIALS BY POSITIVE DISPLACEMENT PUMPS.

(Ah the marram grass, the sand hills of Maioro, the long luminous trek to the sea.)

The slurry pipe crosses the land from Maioro to Glenbrook, from the Waikato River to the Manukau harbour carrying ironsands to Glenbrook steel mill, the used water disposed of into the harbour. The waters of the Waikato mixed with the waters of the Manukau, the spirits of the waters mixed together.

The judge ruled that the Planning Tribunal was required to apply RATIONAL, SCIENTIFIC AND MANAGERIAL TECHNIQUES IN THE MANAGEMENT OF THE NATURAL ENVIRONMENT, THAT PURELY METAPHYSICAL CONCERNS COULD NOT BE TAKEN INTO ACCOUNT.

*

Heading for Pollok, we pass a Maori woman stooped at the roadside gathering puha among the grass and brambles.

I don't know what you expect to find, my uncle's saying. There's not much there. A few cottages, a school, a weatherboard church newly painted as brazenly white as fine weather cumulus, someone mowing a lawn, sunshine like honey.

Imagine you are standing with your back to sombre paintings in gilded frames. From the window, smirr drifts across ruffled branches. You descend the steps of the garden, yourself a point in its perspective. Across the river voices like mist rise from the reeds. The heritor, desiring a pastoral vista, cleared the old township and laid it out to fields. For Pollok is a memory and a dispossession though this is not entered, merely: *Pollok. Auckland Province. Locality Franklin County. Farming. 15 miles north-west by road from Waiuku. Named by pioneer settlers from Pollokshaws, a suburb of Glasgow.*

Beside the road a Waikato woman stoops to gather puha from among the grass and brambles.

For Pollok is a memory and a dispossession though this is not entered.

From a finger of land running northwards to the mouth of the harbour we head downhill. The old wharf, long disused, is a jumble of collapsed slabs slippy with algae. The Manukau stinks at our feet. Across the arm of water the stacks of the steel mill throw up plumes of smoke.

THE PRODUCTION OF STEEL FROM TITANOMAGNETITE SAND IS A WORLD FIRST, AND THIS PLANT AT GLENBROOK, SOUTH AUCKLAND, IS THE ONLY ONE OF ITS TYPE. IT WAS DESIGNED TO USE A PROCESS LARGELY DEVELOPED BY NEW ZEALAND ENGINEERS TO PRODUCE STEEL FROM INDIGENOUS IRONSAND AND SUB-BITUMINOUS COAL – THE BIGGEST SINGLE SITE DEVELOPMENT IN NEW ZEALAND.

Positive displacement, they believed, was a good thing for the country.

*

Godzone	–	God's Own Country
LPG	–	liquid petroleum gas
Whare	–	house
Puha	–	sow thistle

Coral Hull

TARONGA PARK ZOO

They are laughing at the grizzly bear who searches for wild honey in a rock. The giant with the slightly crazy sway was checking out his cage front. He had that desperate painted look of a dog bothered by heat. A billion black flies, deep from a Canadian rocky summer, had entered the ears with their deep hum. This time of the year was a bad life for the bear. A swarm streamed out from the huge angry hive of his head. His old face was bitten by boredom and stress. Later that afternoon I was in Lietchardt and the weather changed. I looked out over Sydney like I had on the ferry away from Taronga Park Zoo. I thought of the hum inside the bear's head. The brain of the bear is corrupted meat. The big heart beat, pounds down like a ship through waves behind the fading fur. I cannot forgive the zoo for that. The whole humid harbour swarms with boats driven crazy by the rich kids, and the middle aged. Taronga Park Zoo locks onto the northern hemisphere animals that have smelt the foreign salt for decades. The wild gulls have flown past the equatorial birds, who are locked onto a space of an artificial rainforest, where the trees are dwarfed and never grow. Even in short flights the birds inside are frozen. They are pinned through the back like moths to a display board. I do not know their names. I only hear their small sad cries. A little bit of hell exists on the crags of Sydney harbour. Spiritually, it's like an open wound, or a big sore gone green. I'm making no apologies for it. The ignorant zoo crowds form the living bars, that keep me from the animal hearts. I'm knocking on the glass of the house of the deaf. The animals are locked onto the flesh of my throat. Two white tigers slept inside an aquarium filled with light. John said, *'did you see the tiger's breath drawing the grass blade in and out like this?'* His little finger fell down like grass. The blade was escaping the great sleep of the tiger. There is a way that this rhythm goes on forever, inside the aquarium that never changes. There is a slow sun travelling across those corners. Clouds, storms, seasons and the moon are travelling across those corners. There is no wind to carry the tiger across its hunting landscapes. There is a sleeping tiger who has to wake up. There is a big cat in a glass tank. It was like a toddler dreaming into a huge blue pillow in a dilapidated building in Redfern. Yet there were the small miracles amongst it. There was the fragile bone of John's finger bending and flexible beneath the flesh. There was a huge white tiger who could shift the position of a grass blade without breaking it. I didn't want to enter the captive tiger's dreams, to say how very sorry I was to be there, and anywhere near this mangy and magical life. In a different tank an Australian sea lion looped the loop. She constructed amazing passageways like children constructing plastic track to zoom their matchbox cars along. She laid down her smooth grey freeways inside a watery space the size of a lift. *The Cure* were a UK pop band who drowned in a closet, as it fell over a cliff face during a video clip. Her heart should have been like the closet that smashed onto rocks that were smashed by the ocean. The Sea World dolphins knew what to do, when they committed suicide by smashing their faces into the sides of concrete pools. Instead this tragic optimist came up to the front of the tank to look at the human bars. Chlorinated water snorted in and out of her whiskered nostril, as she sought some sense and was again disappointed. She was caught between looking for something and giving up. Her eye again glassed over as she twisted tracks through pools. There was an oceanic wilderness inside twisting itself into knots so tight it was heart wrenching. There is a pressure build up along the slippery wharves of circular quay, the hairy ropes burn my fingers red. Suddenly, the big creaking ferries have finally dislodged the quay from Sydney. The green painted boats are on the loose, heading out through The Headlands towards the Pacific Ocean. I will not forgive the zoo for the elephant, for his far fetched torment. His sway and bash in every waking moment and when he slept, he was swaying like those simulated waves inside the Australian sea lion enclosure. The smell of the ocean from the harbour persisted and grew strong before the storm did, whilst those marine mammals twisted in parallel swimming pools, as we caught the ferry further and further and further away. For now, those ferries that circle the harbour and those sea lions that circled the pools. At every cage John said, *'that's the worst.*' It got worse as the day grew longer. I knew that he would not forgive them for what they did to the Andies Condor. '*It's a bird that* SOARS *in high altitudes!*' he said as his words tried to soar, rising up inside his own throat. I could hear the choke of what tethers emotions, and the damp finality of wings that would never meet clouds. A tremendous lonesome bird sat behind layers of wire and pipes, the cage roof rising six foot over its head. Taronga Park Zoo flattened the Andes. They made that condor crawl.

THE MEXICAN GREY WOLF RETURNS TO THE WILD

I am not my childhood anymore. It has gone like a puddle from a street, after a freak thunderstorm. There are dried up areas inside me crying out for rain, hard on the edges, soft in the centres. Drought-affected in my early thirties, I have been no match for the sun. The rain comes in to fill the patches and it floods.

When I try to see where I have come from, everything seems a long way off. It's seven Adelaide beaches away. Telecommunication wires cannot reach that far, only the wind can. There is no use stepping into a coastal phone booth. Screaming rage into currents of hot dry air, is best you can hope to do.

I am turning back for what I have left behind. Imagine being caught in a fire or a flood and leaving yourself there to die. A disaster, my childhood has been destroyed. The last time it happened, there was a nuclear bomb in the loungeroom, glowing softly behind the Venetian blinds, cooking the fishtank.

You left your handbag on a country train and felt panic, your house keys, wallet and a photograph of your past. Somewhere part of you hurtled south to Colac station. Mexican wolves take their first steps from the cage. The female and her nine month old pup return to Arizona, for the first time in decades.

A wolf pad falls on silent earth. They have been here before. This whole land has old wolf songs stored inside it. It has waited for their come back. They have left the zoo and captive breeding program behind. The Apache National Forest extends before them for hundreds of miles. They are small grey dots in space.

In 1976 this great grey wolf had been placed on the endangered species list. Not long after, the last wild lobo seen in that area, was found dead at the southern tip of the Arizona-New Mexico line. The sun bleach-dried the body, whose jaws ate sand. In this country there was enough room and space enough for a wolf.

"I grew up in country," he said. "I always had a sense that something was missing." The Mexican grey wolf is being returned to the wild. A bright eye devours the landscape. Maps of mountains, valleys and rivers with scent as the borders, were already built within them. It is hard to keep from shouting.

CIRCUS TIGER NOT TO BLAME FOR BITING OFF TRAINER'S FOREARM

The Bengal tiger which bit off the arm of a Chipperfield circus keeper Nigel Wessman 32 was not to blame for the incident, its breeder said yesterday. 'The tiger didn't do it. His teeth did it.'

Four-year-old Rajah was in his pen with his sisters, Sita and Rani. Mr Wessman's left forearm was severed below the elbow when he put it into Rajah's cage on Wednesday evening, ignoring the usual procedure of using a metal bar to open a partition and bash the tiger's head in. 'I thought they were my friends,' the distraught Wessman said, 'I trusted them.'

Surgeons who later amputated the limb above the elbow gave Mr Wessman some advice at the hospital, 'You may as well take this with you and feed it to Rajah. It seems like a waste just throwing it away.'

Rajah was bred and beaten up for circus work, and is hired out each summer to European circuses. Circus owner, Mr Turncliffe was confident that the tiger would fulfill this year's engagements with other inexperienced forearms in Belgium.

'Rajah is a very good natured tiger who loves the trainers who beat him, and there is no reason to think that he will be too full, to cope with future forearms offered to him,' he said.

'He probably thought that Mr Wessman was feeding him, with himself. It's not uncommon for tiger trainers to have this kind of personal commitment to the animals.

As far as I'm concerned Wesson is an experienced tiger keeper. He was also very brave, telling everyone to calm down, whilst he gently coaxed Rajah to let go of his jugular.

Anyway, I really don't see how we can blame the tiger for this incident. It's a completely humane method of removing a circus trainer's forearm. It was just one of those things, over in a couple of seconds.'

Wessmans's wife added to this, saying, 'Nigel was very brave. He simply placed his forearm in my handbag on the way to the hospital. It was a bit gross, like carrying a dog's bone home from the butchers without the wrapping. But I did it for him.'

A portable television normally watched by the tigers in the evenings, featuring a local advertisement for TCP lozenges with a tiger biting a man's throat out, was later withdrawn from the cages.

BRONX ZOO

~wildlife will escape the zoo~

if you become a zoo keeper, the wild that you think you keep will escape you, in anyway it knows how, it will gnaw its own limbs off to be rid of you, it will leave its own body behind in your hands in order to escape you, that is what i found inside the prison of the bronx zoo, the thing that was confined behind the bars was the physical body, it was what the animal had left behind, the best that the animal could do, was to float above its body that had become a cell within a cell, the zoo keeper is left with a bad conscience, the public is left with uneasiness, regardless of the publicity machine, wildlife will escape the zoo in any way it knows how to, some animals had died and were free,

~the world of birds~

it was a bright blue backdrop, with no sky to think of, the world of birds was like allowing a child to walk on a glass floor above a beach, and watching them trying to dip their hands down into the waves, i entered the world of birds as a cry broke loose from a rainforest bird, crying out to nothing but painted walls and a fake sky, it was as if that cry had released the same cry in me, the cry kept up perpetually and the same, until i knew that bird to be insane, the carmine bee eater from tropical africa, sits beneath a skylight, in the wild it forages while in flight, colonies may in hundreds and thousands, it rides large animals in order to catch insects, inside the sunless world of birds, another call echoes out beneath the skylight, the desperate trumpet of montezuma oropendula from mexico, central america, in this sound my despair, the future of us all,

~glowing scorpion~

there was this poor scorpion, huddled in a dirty corner of a glass tank, with no sting left in it, when you pressed a button on the panel, the tank rocks turned purple, and the scorpion glowed fluorescent green, to show us its miserable hiding spot, i imagine that scorpions hate to be revealed, and there it was in its dead little world, in his dead little tank, in its dead little heart, bright fluorescent green at the touch of a button, courtesy of the same country, that had lit up the niagara falls, turning it into disney land,

~the elephant is so slow~

'*hadie, hadie ho, the great big elephant is so slow, she swings her trunk from side to side, as she takes the children for a ride, hadie, hadie hoe, the elephant is so slow,*' i was riding on the back of the poor old elephant at taronga park zoo as a child, she had been made into a childless mother, her calves sold off to other zoos, as a girl i had been taught to sing that song in school, but I didn't want to ride her, and was frightened as she paced her endless circle, the zoo worker gathering children, and placing them into a brightly painted wooden float behind her ears, she spent her long life dragging her chains, this feeling of tremendous anguish consumed me, it was bigger than my life had been, a lot of the kids were crying when the ride had finished, the adults saying, '*never mind, did she frighten you did she?,*'

~a world without animals~

a grey wolf looked through the broken planks, it could have smelt us several snow covered kilometres away, now it was mangy and bored, depressed, pacing, not fit for a domestic dog, not a wolf anymore, imagine a world without animals, or where they only existed in zoos, big, smart and sociable to nil, the bronx zoo is a zoo within a zoo, squashed in between freeways and subways, the tenement buildings creeping over the trees, neighbours peeking at animals from between the gunshots and the curtains, it made them feel better about their own lives, the concrete in the bear pit is painted white, to remind the psychotic polar bear of the arctic, whilst it completely rejected the artificial environment that had been made for it, there was a 4 month old giraffe trying to eat the vegetation painted on the wall, this is a world without animals, and we were meant to preserve our wildlife memories by taking a photo there,

~the snow lions~

the bronx zoo doesn't provide plastic lids or straws, because people throw them at the animals, perhaps to get the animals' attention or to make contact, the woman who works in the cafeteria said, '*they lost several animals on plastic lids,*' i didn't ask them what ones, it could have been the so and so or the so and so, until i write about every animal choking and the whole zoo chokes on plastic, the captive snow lions cling to one another in their small world, as far as they are concerned they are the last snow lions left on earth, they have never heard the cry of another snow lion, or of another species that might have shared their ecosystem, in their many years of sitting and pacing, they twitch through nightmares that only a snow lion could have, we have no chance in entering the minds of them, please do not throw coins or plastic lids into the pool, there is nothing left to wish for,

~the reptile house~

the snake was out in the galaxy, a boelens python that lay wrapped around itself, drugged from slow heat, its slight breath, its dead black eye is something i'll never forget, jen said, '*it's out of its body*,' the fluro light twinkled on its pupil that saw nothing from its capture on, the chinese alligator was distressed, the common snapping turtle had been facing black glass since 1995, caught in Paul Skill river, New Jersey, it was as excited as a child facing a wall, then there was the Cuban crocodile, known for its temper and jumping attacks, obviously he didn't want the little fountain the zoo had made him, 'samantha' was a 22 ft reticulated python 'rescued' from hide hunters, she had become a breathing carpet, lastly the lace monitor and goanna, we wanted to take them with us and let them go, back home in australia,

~what I saw was distress~

the bronx zoo calls itself the 'wildlife conservation society,' what I saw was the work of a rich and unethical director, controller of the dumb volunteers who didn't seem to know any better, and a zoo keeper who whistled louder than the birds, what i saw was a single polar bear clearly disturbed, pacing, swaying, throwing its back legs out, like it walked with a thorn in its heart, i saw two porcupines, one lying still like an old rock painting, the other pacing, trying to walk into an environment that wasn't there, then battering its body against the wall, in the worlds of darkness an egyptian fruitbat's wings pierced several fake branches, as it made another attempt to launch itself into orbit, it fell from the air like a kite and scrambled,

~north american otter~

what i saw was an otter pacing, twirling in and out of the water, in forgotten river number eights, crazy, frustrated, this too far gone for too long north american, racing around a shape, circling its own neck, reptilian mammal, in constant motion, in self combat and self defeat, twisting with no relationship to anything, in comparison to the dreadful comments from the public, '*oh, look he's showing off*,' what I saw was two blue black pumas in a 10ft by 8ft glass enclosure, one sitting, the other pacing a dead log, the log cat had completely lost it, as if having now travelled so far out of its body, that i'm sure that if it looked back down, it would be stunned to hear its own heart beating,

~mask of the ape~

imagine being locked in room with five people for the rest of your life, i hung my head before the western low land gorilla, before clashing with her eyes, at the edge of the enclosure, she said '*there is no nature*,' and challenged me to tell her otherwise, her family had to urinate in front of us, all I could say was '*i'm sorry*', into her crazy mask and slight sway, they look at you as if you are an absolute fuckwit, they are unforgiving, sucking on straw, fed up, older ones showing the stress, thirty five gorillas born in the bronx zoo since 1972, trees disappear into the concrete, as a painted on community, with the wrong shaped leaves, next door there is a grid floor for the white checked gibbon, trunks that never grow and never die, moss coloured paint, the zoo has its answers for everything, plastic plants, the smell of mildew, and they knew, those staff, those volunteers, that sadistic zoo director animal collector, he knew too,

POEMS

BARBARA NICGRIOGAIR / BABS MACGREGOR

QIAO JIFU / BRIAN HOLTON

PIER PAOLO PASOLINI / CHRISTOPHER WHYTE / ALEXANDER HUTCHISON / CARLA SASSI / LAURA FIORENTINI / TOM SCOTT

KING HALA / ANDREW SCHELLING

FOUR ARVANIT POEMS / PETER CONSTANTINE

NUALA NÍ DHOMHNAILL / KAARINA HOLLO

Three Poems

Barbara Nicgriogair / Babs Macgregor

'sous le trottoir il y a la plage' / 'underneath the pavement there is the beach'
– mai '68

AN GAIDHEAL / THE PAKISTANI

1

anns gach baile brònach / *in every mournful city*
fo'n a' phavement fiadhaich / *underneath pavements growing wild*
tha tràigh 'gad ionndrainn / *there is a beach that longs for you*
bata na do làmh / *a walking stick in your hand*
bata na do shùilean / *a boat in your eyes*

2

neapaicean geala / *a white handkerchief*
mar isean air an iteig / *like a bird on the wing*
an dé aig a' phort-adhair / *yesterday at the airport*
an diugh na do phòcaid / *today in your pocket*

tha an saoghal a' fàs nas lugha / *the world is growing smaller*
's an tigh nas motha / *and the house bigger*
tha an clann a' fàs mor / *the children are growing up*
'gad fhàgail le fotos is telebhisean / *leaving you with photographs and television*

ceann air a' bhalla neo ann am bocsa / *a head on a wall or on a box*
ann an leabhar neo ann an sgàthan / *in a book or in a mirror*

cumaidh tu air, le na soithichean 's le na sgothan / *you will keep on with the dishes and the clouds*
an sion nad chùlaibh / *the rain at your back*
seòladair nan speuran / *sailor of the skies*

3

eadar breith is bàs tha B&B ann an Glaschu / *between births and deaths there is a B&B in Glasgow*
eadar prìs chaoraich is prìs chrodh tha caitheamh-beatha / *between the price of sheep and that of cattle there is a livelihood*
eadar clach is cladh tha cuimhne / *between a stone and a grave there is a memory*

4

tha goirt 's an tìr / *famine is in the land*
is pian 'nad amhaich / *and a pain is in your throat*
tha blas canain / *the taste of a language*
fhathast air do theanga / *lingers on the tongue*
's an t- acras ort / *and you are hungry*

5

le leac-uaghach an àite chluasig / *with a tombstone for a pillow*
chan fhaigh thu móran chadail / *you won't get much sleep*
air do ghlùinean ann an cidsin / *on your knees in a kitchen*
neo ann an achadh / *or in a field*
ach seasaidh do chreideamh / *with your faith still standing.*

AN DUINE DUBH / THE HIGHLANDER

dachaidh air do dhruim / *a home on your back*
bùth air do bhaidhseagail / *a shop on your bicycle*
fosgladh tu do mhaileid / *you would open your suitcase*
gaire lan grein. 'Seall seo!' / *with a smile as wide as sunshine. 'Look at this!'*

***lingerie* in lingerbay** / *lingerie in lingerbay*
sìoda ann an làmhan chruaidh a' chroiteir / *silk in the rough hands of a crofter*
sìol ùr bho fad as / *new seed from far away*
cho aotrum, cho aluinn / *so light, so beautiful*

a' siubhal am measg strainnsearan / *travelling among strangers*
cothromaichte le feansaichean is cinn-theagaisg / *weighted down by fenceposts and texts*
cha robh 'nad cheum / *only memory and homesickness*
ach cuimhne is cianalas / *to dog your step*

a'bàsachachadh leis an fhuachd / *catching your death of cold*
reic thu d'aodaich / *you sold your clothes*
's thog thu teine, tigh is teaghlach / *and you built a fire, a house and raised a family*
an diugh tha do bhùitean lan dhaoine / *today your shops are full of people*
's do mhaileid a' feitheamh / *and your suitcase is waiting*
tha na laithean saora a' fas nas daora / *the holidays are getting dearer*
a nis nach eil ach deilbh a thogail / *now there are only photographs to take*

SAILM / SALAAM PSALM / PEACE

sailm
salaam
clearance
sail
mecca
bingo
àireamh / *a number*
ainm / *a name*
gabh curam / *take care*
mo ghràidh / *my love*
air do chothrom / *of your opportunity*
's air do chridhe / *and of your love*
brisidh la ùr / *a new day will break*
mar aran / *like bread*
's togaidh sinn na crumaichean gu n-ar beul / *and we will lift the crumbs to our mouths*
's gabhaidh sinn taing / *and we will give thanks*
sailm
salaam

Anent Luve

bi Qiao Jifu: owreset bi Brian Holton

TI THE AIR O '*TRAIVLIN OAMS*'

dowie the swalla, wae the gowdspink
burdalane the phoenix, hert-alane his marra
luve's no lang o dwynin awa
cruppen-in like shilpit Dongyang
lyart grey like auld Pan Yue
A'm feart for spring's retour
A wearie at enless days
an gley at failin nichts

TI THE AIR O '*HANDSEL O HARMONIE*'

ance dawtit wi play mang the lassies
no like the nou
salt jades an warm perfumes ill ti seek
juist in dwaums nou, A dout
juist in dwaums

TI THE AIR O '*FLOUERS ON BROCADE*'

poet's poupit, bouzer's queir
nae mait, nae drink
doul i the wame, ondings i thenicht
easlin winds, begrutten een
vous like the muckle sea, hechtins like the hills
a chein o pure white jade
the mune trystit wi a staur
a wee bit screed o pouthert gowd

TI THE AIR O '*THE WEE SWIRE*'

ane an bi ane bricht munes eclipse
hoolie an slaw the clouds skail
A'm an inch awa frae the halie hill
than instanter awa yont the border
yirth's gey an narra tho the heivens is braid
an A've ettled at it owre an owre
but luve's clouds is wersh, rains few an faur atween
an there's ills ti come bi the thousan

TI THE AIR O '*RIVER WATTER*'

A've leaned at ilka doorcheek i the Wastlin Touer
lang sicherins tuim whaur howp's aa tint
A'm no on hecklepins for her fuit
ma hert's skeerie tae, nae dout
but A'll lee about it whan A see her

TI THE AIR O '*WHUSSLE O GREEN JADE*'

she thinks
idletie stown frae the thrang
tein an sorra's aa at's in ma mou
here ablow or in heiven
swires an bens sinder us
ye'll can see in ma een ma hert is his
niver a word ti say, ma face as lang's ma hair

he thinks
a braw an a rantin style
pouthert an paintit same as iver
jimp-waistit wee deivil at she is
her clavers bonnie as the gowdspink i the spring

TI THE CODA '*RESTIN FRAE THE FOY I THE LUDGE*'

aa ma days A niver cud win free o wildness
this year A've rin ramstam ance mair on the hechle o the rantin life
it's easie seen there's a catch ti't aa

bed-claes idle   luvebirds on the broidert haps
hairpreins gane in twa   phoenix on gowden flouers
strings snappit   wildgeese on a beriall clarsach
a saft heft dowie at the hint o hairst
ill-daein een wearie for the caller dawin

whae's ti ken at nearhaun by
roukie watters   owre the Blue Brig pourin
luve's clouds an rain   on Eildon's heuchs aa drouthie
hert-hunger deep   an Schiehallion muckle
luve gane ti smush   stane spleit wi firtree ruits

it wisna me at dafft wi you
eggd yon younker on
gart ye lou anither

Poems

Pier Paolo Pasolini

Preface to the Pasolini Translations

These translations of Pasolini's poetry should be read in conjunction with the essays by Carla Sassi and Stuart Hood and the review by Mark Cousins which appear later in this issue. Pasolini's films have been very influential within twentieth-century cinema, but it is his poetry upon which the *Review* is focused, with translations by Tom Scott and Alexander Hutchison of his early lyric poems (1944-49), written originally in Pasolini's mother-tongue, the Friulian dialect, a factor reflected in their rustic settings. Two of the poems, 'The Rose Lintie' and 'Swank as a Shalt', appear in four-way Friulian/Italian/Scots/English translations and glosses. There is a move in the long poem 'The Lament of the Mechanical Digger' (translated by Christopher Whyte), from the country to the city – a move which is reflected in Pasolini's own biography, as the boy from the country became an urban man, a film director as well as a poet. Despite the shift in settings, a constant theme remains, highlighted in the opening poem of this section, 'Le Litanie del bel Ragazzo', translated by Tom Scott, with its use of the figure of the 'braw lad', the *ragazzo* or young man, a figure which recurs throughout his poetry and indeed his film-making.

Le Litanie del bel Ragazzo

I

Winter's here, the cricket sang
And we hear it can be suir
Aathing is baith clear and strang.
Aa doun here is hevin's bliss –
Isnae that whit we find here?
Rain, cloud, pain o hell's abyss.

II

I'm a braw lad indeed
and aa day I greet and plead
O Jesus keep me
frae a mool wi the deid.

Jesus Jesus Jesus.

I'm a braw lad indeed
and aa day I lauch and plead
that you, Jesus, gie me
a guid mool wi the deid.

Jesus Jesus JESUS.

Translated by Tom Scott.

The Dinnle O Bells

Fan the gloamin's fizzelt oot in the fountains
it raivels the toonlan licht.

Awa an awa, I can mine on: puddocks,
meen-bow, trist trimmilin o crickets.

Vespers ding an dwinnle in the rigs:
a'm deid t' the dinnle o bells.

Ootlan, dinna be feart,
in ma canny flicht ower the skelp

I'm a spreit o luve
fidgin hame fae hyne awa.

Gloamin is twilight; *toonlan* is townland; *raivelt* is confused, uncertain; *mine on* is remember; *puddocks* are frogs; *meen-bow*: the moon sometimes has a bow; *trist* is sad, *crickets* are crickets (but in Scots they're grasshoppers too); *rigs* are ploughed strips of land; *dinnle* is a peal; *ootlan* is a stranger; *feart* is afraid; *canny* here is steady, gentle, pleasant; *skelp* a long stretch or expanse of ground; *fidgin* is excited, eager; *hyne awa* is far away.

Translated by Alexander Hutchison

Furth An Awa

Ye quid get
a richt fleg
noo, gawkin
ahint the days
fan I wis a birkie
– aye, the virra loon
that's nae me noo,
an herks t' the houlat
spirkin in a laun
that naebody sees.

Ye quid gie
a richt skellich
noo, caain t' mine
fit's ill t' kinnle
– the een o a birkie
Buckie loon, wi nae
tears or nithin t' faa –
an the merkits
bummin in ma heid
lik it's nae ma ain.

Ye quid gie
a richt deid-chack
noo, wi the leesome
an caller airs
o Buchan braes
caa'd thegither in
a blue blink o days
– nae tint, bit nae oors
aither – scuddie in a
yokin soonless as licht.

Furth an awa is out, or outside, and away (Pasolini's title "De Loinh" is not Friulian but Provençal); *richt fleg* is a real fright; *gawkin* is peering, staring; *ahint* is behind; *fan* is when; *birkie* refers here to a smart, well-built youth or boy; *virra loon* is the very boy; *herks* is harks, listens; *houlet* (or oolet) is an owl; *spirkin* is sparking, lively; *laun* is land; *skellich* is a shrill cry; *caain t' mine* is calling to mind, remembering; *fit* is what; *ill t' kinnle* is hard to light; *een* are eyes; *faa* is fall; *merkits* refers to feeing or hiring markets, often combined with fairs; *bummin* is ringing, echoing; *nae ma ain* is not my own; *deid-chack* here is a noise as the premonition of death; *leesome* is bright, fine, pleasant; *caller* is fresh (Pasolini's "hot" and "cold" is a more direct contrast); *caa'd thegither* is mixed or brought together; *tint* is lost, or gone beyond recall; *oors aither* is ours either; *scuddie* is naked; *yokin* is a yoking, joining together, but also a stint, or shift of work; *soonless* is silent, soundless.

Translated by Alexander Hutchison

Il lújar

No il sanc no il cuàrp,
amòur, no ti ciantavin,
al ti ciantava il lújar
murínt ta la rèit.

No il sanc no no il cuàrp,
amòur, no ti planzèvin,
al ti planzeva il lújar
murínt ta la rèit.

No il sanc no il cuàrp,
amòur, no ti sigàvin,
al ti sigava il lújar
ridínt tal sèil.

IL LUCHERINO. Non il sangue, non il corpo, amore, ti cantavano, ti cantava il lucherino morendo nella rete.

Non il sangue, non il corpo, amore, ti piangevano, ti piangeva il lucherino morendo nella rete.

Non il sangue, non il corpo, amore, ti gridavano, ti gridava il lucherino, ridendo nel cielo.

The Rose Lintie

Nae the bleed, nae the body,
jo, were chirmin o you –
the lintie wis chirmin o you,
deein in the wyve.

Nae the bleed, nae the body,
jo, were murnin for you,
the lintie wis murnin for you,
deein in the wyve.

Nae the bleed, nae the body,
jo, were keenin ower you –
the lintie wis keenin for you,
skirlin i' the lift.

The *rose lintie* is the male linnet in bright red courting plumage (Pasolini's *lujar* is a siskin – close enough); *bleed* is blood; *jo* is love or sweetheart; *chirmin* is warbling, chittering; *deein* is dying; *wyve* is the weave of a net; *murnin* is mourning, weeping; *skirling* is laughing, as well as crying out shrilly; *lift* is sky.

Translated by Alexander Hutchison

Bel coma un ciaval

Me pare al me à dat thento franchi:
vinti ani, bel coma un ciaval,
ardi de festi e de ligrii.

Al cine al bal a li ligrii,
fiesta, te meni el ciaval;
vita, te costi thento franchi.

Mi ridi cui me thento franchi
cui rith e i vuoj rossi de ligrii
e li nothenthi dal ciaval.

Siòrs, ve costi thento franchi.

BELLO COME UN CAVALLO. Mio padre mi ha dato cento lire: venti anni,
bello come un cavallo, splendo di feste e di allegrie.

Al cine, al ballo, alle allegrie, festa, tu conduci il cavallo; vita, costi cento lire.

Rido con le mie cento lire, coi ricci e gli occhi rossi di allegrie e le innocenze del cavallo.

Ricchi, vi costo cento lire.

Swank as a Shalt

The aul man's gien's a hunner tackets:
twinty year aul, swank as a shalt,
hot t' trot at flings an fairs.

At the picters, an jiggin, oot blin billy,
it's crouse, it's curcuddy, ee lowse the shaltie:
life, it'll cost ye ten big eens.

I keckle on wi my ten smackers:
twirly haffets, een reid wi rantin,
an the wytelessness o the pownie.

Aa you plutocrats, the ticket's ten poun.

The *aul man* here means father; *gien's* is given me (though it refers to the plural form 'us'); *a hunner tackets* (a hundred hobnails) turns out to be ten pounds. *Swank* is lithe, agile, strong; *shalt, sheltie or shaltie* is a Shetland pony: stocky and full of vitality. Pasolini's beautiful horse in 'Bel com un ciaval' conveys something of Whitman's marvellous lines: 'haughty, proud, electrical – I and this mystery here we stand': but the Scots 'cuddie' or 'horsie' don't quite fit, and I opted for the spirited 'shalt', accepting the difference in scale. *Oot blin billy* is a mix of things, but *blin* is blind, *billy* can be a lover, a term of endearment, and the phrase suggests being out on a spree; *crouse* is confident, spirited; *curcuddy* is a low crouching dance; *ee* is *you*; *lowse* is loose; *big eens* are big ones; *keckle* is cackle, laugh loudly: *haffets* are side locks of hair; *reid een* are red eyes; *rantin* is partying; *wytelessness* is innocence, blamelessness; *pownie* is a pony; *aa* is all.

Translated by Alexander Hutchison

Reivers

In ticht at yer mither's
can ye still fin
on yer lips the kisses
I rypit lik a reiver?

Aye, baith o's herriers!
Wis't nae richt mirk i' the meadie?
Streckit on yon tattie-poke
did we nae sneck the shadda aff the roddens?

Nae fother for
the rubbits the nicht –
an your pykit lips
preed til the first starn...

Reive, *herry*, *rype*, *pike* and *sneck* are all words meaning to sneak, rob or steal; *in ticht* is in tight – with the sense of close or snug; *fin* is to feel or sense; *mirk* is dark; *meadie* or *meedie* is meadow; *streckit* is stretched out; *yon* is that; *tattie-poke* a sack; *shadda* is shadow; *roddens* are rowan trees; *fother* is fodder (grass is used in the original); *the nicht* is tonight; *preed* is pursed for a kiss; *til* is to; *starn* a star.

Translated by Alexander Hutchison

Lament of the Mechanical Digger

Pier Paolo Pasolini

(1)

Only loving, only
knowing counts, not having
loved or known. Living

a burnt-out love brings
anguish. The soul stops growing.
Here below, where night, unchecked, between

the curving river, and the drowsy
visions of the city strewn with lights,
still echoes, thousand-lived;

see: in her enchanted heat,
unlove, mystery and sensual
despair render the world's forms,

till yesterday my reason for living,
hateful to me. Tired and bored,
I take my way home through

black market squares, sad streets
around the river port, between
shacks and warehouses mingling with

the last fields. There the silence
is deadly: but down by Viale Marconi,
by the station of Trastevere, the evening

still seems kind. On scooters,
in overalls or dungarees, but urged
by holiday fervour, the lads return

to city wards and housing estates: their friends,
laughing and dirty, ride pillion
behind. The last few customers

stand chatting at the tops of their voices
here and there in the night, at little
tables in bars half-empty, but brilliant still.

Stupendous, miserable city,
you taught me what men learn,
ferocious and cheerful, as children,

small things in which the magnitude of life
is peaceably disclosed: such as, to walk
tough, at the ready through the chaos of

the streets, turn to another man without
trembling, be unashamed to check
the change the bus conductor counts

with lazy fingers, sweating
against façades that hurry by
in an eternal summer colour;

to defend myself, offend, and have
the world before my eyes, not only
in my heart, to understand

that few men know the passions
I have lived in: that they're not
brothers to me, or brothers

precisely because they have
the passions of men who live,
cheerful, whole, unaware,

from experiences foreign to me.
Stupendous, miserable city,
you gave me experience

of that hidden existence,
to the point where I discovered
what, in each man, was the world.

Expiring in her parasite, the silence,
a moon whitens among violent flares,
that wretchedly, on the earth dumb of life,

blind, with the splendid avenues,
the ancient lanes, but give no light:
the silence mirrors back, in all the world,

a few strands of warm cloud.
This is the summer's finest night.
Reeking of emptied taverns,

of straw from old stables, Trastevere
is wakeful still. In dark
corners, on placid party walls,

magical sounds re-echo.
Below festoons of solitary lights
young and old men turn homewards

to alleyways that rubbish and darkness block,
with those bland steps
that invaded my soul the more

when really I did love, really
I did want to understand.
And, as then, they vanish singing.

(2)

Poor as a Coliseum cat, I lived
in a slum on the outskirts, all dust
and whitewash, far from the city

and from the countryside, squeezed
every day into a spluttering bus:
each outward journey, each return

a calvary of sweat and anxiety.
Long trekking through a tepid haze,
long dusts bent over papers heaped

on the table, among streets of mud, low walls,
small houses coated in whitewash, with
curtains for doors, and no window-frames...

The ragman would come by, the olive man,
from some other estate, their merchandise
thick with dust and looking as if it had

been stolen, their faces cruel, youths
grown old amid the sins of those
with hardened, hungry mothers.

Renewed by the new world,
free – a flame, a breath
I cannot tell, gave the reality,

humble and filthy, confused and huge,
swarming in these outskirts full of southerners,
a sense of serene piety.

A soul in me, not mine alone,
a small soul in that limitless world,
grew then, nurtured by the joy

of one who loved, even if not loved in turn.
This love illuminated everthing.
Maybe still boyish, heroic, yet

tempered by an experience born
at history's feet. I was
at the world's centre, in that world

of savage, miserable suburbs,
acres of yellowing grass forever scoured
by a wind that knew no peace,

whether it came from the hot sea
at Fiumicino, or from the first fields where
the city straggled out among the hovels;

a world that, square and livid
spectre in the livid gloom, riddled
with a thousand rows of indistinguishable

grated windows, between old fields
and dozing farmhouses, only
the Penitentiary could dominate.

Dust and litter carried here and there
by the blind breeze, the poor
unresonant voices of small women from

the Sabine hills, the Adriatic coast,
who'd come and set up camp here,
now with swarms

of hardened, undernourished little boys,
shrieking in tattered vests
and grey, sun-bleached short trousers,

African suns, downpours that
reduced the streets to muddy torrents,
buses at the terminus foundering

in a corner between one last
ribbon of white grass and
some burning, acid midden...

it was the centre of the world,
as my love for it was at
history's centre: and in this maturity

which, though inchoate, was still love,
everything was on the verge
of clarity – was,

clear! That suburb naked in the wind,
not Roman, or southern,
or working-class, was life

in its most immediate light:
life, and light of life, teeming
in a chaos not yet proletarian

(as the crude newsheet of the local
party cell, the latest fluttering of
the cyclostyle would have it): bone

of day-to-day existence,
pure because only too close
at hand, absolute because

only too miserably human.

(3)

I head for home now, rich with those years so green
I'd never have thought to find them old
in a soul remote from them, remote

from any past. Climbing
the avenues on the Janiculum,
I halt at a liberty crossroads, at a brief

and tree-lined square, at a relict of
old walls – on the city's edge by now,
where a rolling plain opens onto the sea.

And in my soul – inert and dark
as the night abandoned to its fragrance –
seeds overripe now to still give fruit

regerminate, in the medley of a life
turned bitter and weary again...
Here's Villa Pamphili and, in the light

serenely cast on new walls,
the street I live in.
Near my house, on a piece of grass

reduced to a dim slavering,
an outline on the chasms freshly
dug in the volcanic rock – all

destructive anger past – rears against
sporadic blocks of flats and scraps of sky,
inanimate, a mechanical digger...

What pain is it that fills me at the sight
of these prostrate implements, scattered
here and there in the mud, of this

red canvas hanging from a trestle in
the corner where the night seems most unhappy?
Why does my conscience offer

such blind resistance to this colour
of faded blood, why hide as if from an
obsessive regret saddening her every recess?

Why is there in me the same sense
of days eternally unfulfilled
as in the dead firmament

the digger is whitening against?

I undress in one of a thousand rooms
in Via Fonteiana where people sleep.
You can dig down to everything, time:

hopes, passions. But not to these
pure forms of life. Man is
brought back to them, when experience

and trust in the world are
brimming... Oh, days at Rebibbia,
I believed you lost in a light of necessity,

and now know you're so free!

Along with my heart, then, through
the troublesome events that had waylaid
its journey towards a human destiny,

making up in fervour for its lack
of clarity, in ingenuousness
for lack of equilibrium – the mind

too, in those days, attained clarity
and equilibrium. And that blind regret,
mark of every struggle I've had

with the world, was repulsed by, yes,
adult though inexpert ideologies...
no longer an enigma, the world became

a matter of history.
The joy of knowing it –
as every man does, humbly –

was increased thousandfold.
Marx, Gobetti, Gramsci, Croce
came to life in lived experience.

The stuff of ten years of obscure
vocation changed, if I devoted myself
to clarifying the image that seemed most

ideal to an ideal generation:
that fervour, that presumption,
that gratitude were in every page,

in every line I wrote in my
exile at Rebibbia. New
in my new condition of

old work and old privation,
the few friends who came to see me
on mornings or evenings

forgotten on the Penitentiary,
saw me within a vivid light:
meek, violent revolutionary in

my heart and in my speech. A man in flower.

(4)

He hugs me against his ageing coat,
that smells of woods, and puts
his muzzle with its great boar's teeth,

or wandering bear's, and a breath of roses, to
my mouth: and the room around me is a clearing,
the bedcover, corroded by my last

juvenile sweatings, dances like a haze
of pollen... And I am in fact
walking along a road that leads

through the first fields of spring, dissolved
in a heavenly light...
Carried by the momentum of my steps,

I leave behind me, wretched, insubstantial,
not the periphery of Rome: '*Viva Mexico*!'
is chalked or scratched on ruined temples,

on low walls at road forks, decrepit,
light as bone at the limits of
a burning and untrembling sky.

Look, on a hilltop where the rise
and fall of an old Appenine range
mingles with the clouds, the town,

half empty, though it is the time
of morning when women come out to shop
– or the evening hour that gilds

children running out of the school
playgrounds with their mothers.
A great quiet invades the streets:

old as time, grey as time,
the slightly parted flagstones peter out
and two long strips of stone,

shiny and dull, run down the streets.
Someone moves in that quiet:
an old woman, a small

boy lost in his games, where
a gentle Renaissance opens serene
portals, or a small well stands

on the skimpy grass in some forgotten
corner or at a crossroads, tiny
animals carved on its rim.

At the top of the hill the lonely
village square opens out, and between
one house and the next, beyond a low

wall and a great, green chestnut tree,
the wide valley can be seen: no valley, but
a volume quivering sky-blue, or only

just milky... The main street continues beyond
that familiar little square suspended in
the Apennine sky, squeezes past

narrower houses, descends briefly
along the slope: and further down
– when the baroque houses thin out –

see, the valley appears – and the waste.
Only a few more steps towards
the curve, where the road already passes

little fields, bare, steep and bristling.
On the left, against the slope,
as though the church had crumbled,

an apse is erect, crowded with frescoes,
red and blue, and thronged with scrolls
along the cancelled scars

of the collapse – which it alone
has survived, an immense shell
gaping against the sky.

It's there, beyond the valley, from the waste,
a breeze starts blowing, light and hopeless,
that kindles the skin with gentleness...

Like the smells blown on the city
from the freshly dampened fields
or from some river's banks

in the first days of fine weather:
you can't identify them, but
crazed almost with regret you try to guess

if they come from a bonfire lit on the frost,
or from grapes and medlars lost in some
granary the stupendous morning

sun is warming.
I shout for joy, struck
so deep in my lungs by that breeze

that, watching the valley, I breathe in
some form of heat or light
....

(5)

A moment's peace suffices to reveal
the heart's anguish, limpid
as the seabed on a day

of sunshine. Though you don't feel,
you recognize the ill of it,
chest, thighs and feet

sprawled in the bed there, as if
crucified – or like Noah, drunk
and dreaming, naively unaware

of the gaiety of sons who,
strong and pure, ridicule him...
by now the day is upon you,

like a sleeping lion in the room.

By what roads does the heart
come to be full, perfect even in this
mixture of blessedness and pain?

A moment's peace... And war, and God
awake in you again. The passions
are scarcely relaxed, the fresh wound

is scarcely closed, and already you're
expending a soul that seemed completely spent
in dream actions that yield

nothing... Look, if kindled to hope
– because, old lion stinking of vodka,
Krushchev from his offended Russia

swears to the world – *look,*
you realise you're dreaming.
Each passion, each of your

interior torments, each
naive shame at not being
– in feeling – where the world's

renewed, seems to burn
in this happy August of peace.
More than that, this new

breath of wind chases you back
to where all winds abate: where,
self-regenerating tumour, you

encounter love's old crucible again,
the sense, the fear, the joy.
And precisely in that somnolence

lies the light... purity in that
infantile unawareness, an animal's
or an ingenuous libertine's... the most

heroic rages in that flight, the most
divine sensation in that lowly human
act perpetrated in my morning sleep.

(6)

In the abandoned glare
of the morning sun – flaying
the workyards now, burning fiercely

on scalded window frames –
desperate vibrations scrape the silence
that reeks hopelessly of old milk,

small empty squares and innocence.
Since seven at the latest that vibration
has mounted with the sun. A dozen old

labourers are pitifully here,
with tattered clothes and singlets burnt
with sweat, their infrequent voices,

their struggles against scattered blocks
of mud and earth-flows seeming
to break up in that tremor.

But between the swinging shovel's sudden
outbursts – seeming blind, it blindly
crumbles, blindly grips, as if

its gestures had no aim,
a sudden, human cry emerges,
and returns at intervals,

so mad with pain it at once stops sounding
human, and goes back to being an
inanimate screech. Then, slowly,

it's rebegotten in the violent light,
among the sightless blocks of flats,
new, the same, a cry only a man

dying could utter in his final instant
beneath this sun that still shines cruelly,
already mellowed by a breath from the sea...

Lacerated by months
and years of morning
sweat – accompanied

by her mute litter of lesser masons,
it's the old mechanical digger shouting:
but with it, the freshly violated earth

or, within the brief limits of the twentieth-
century horizon, the whole district...
It is the city, slumped in a festive clarity

– the world. What ends and starts again
is crying. What was once a stretch of grass,
an open space, and now will be

a wax-white back-court, shut
in a decorum that is rancour;
what was almost an old fair of fresh

plaster askew in the sun, and will be
a new block, teeming in
an order that is deadened pain.

What changes, even if for the better,
is crying. Not for a single
instant does the light of the future cease

to hurt us: it's here, burning
in our every daily act,
anguish even in the confidence

that gives us life, in the Gobettian
impulse towards these workmen, dumbly raising
in the ward of the opposing human camp

their red rag of hope.

1956

translated by Christopher Whyte

Poems from the *Sattasai* of King Hala

Andrew Schelling

How many loves
we took
into those cane groves
the black bees also coming and going
But dear friend I'm afraid
time has left
on the riverbank
only dry stalks

– *anonymous*

Sattasai 5.22

Night after night in the
rainy season
I'd push my way
through village mud to your door
the mud is no different today
but how
cold you have grown
how ungrateful

– *anonymous*

Sattasai 5.45

Eyes closed
she imagines leading him
into her bed
she touches her own breasts adoringly
on her arms
the loose bangles

– *anonymous*

Sattasai 2.33

It was like
touching the tenderest
dew-covered petals
the hundred intimate places she
guided my hands
Or was night just a dream?
today she tosses
her head and won't
look at me

Makaranda

Sattasai 1.23

He gets up from
the mat
after we make love
and steps into the moonlight –
just for a moment
it's as though he's vanished into
some unimaginably
far off country

Makaranda

Sattasai 1.98

She tells herself
he is coming
and night's first watch
flashes away like a shooting star
but in the hours
from midnight till dawn
the girl ages
a full year

Ardhra

Sattasai 4.85

Don't go down
for flowers
to Godavari river
our village gods only ask
a handful of water in offering
petals crushed on a secret
lovebed
don't please them

Nandara

Sattasai 4.55

Crows wheel and fly up
from the riverbank
caw caw
they saw where the girl
was deflowered

Addhandra Raja

Sattasai 3.18

Shiva tears off
Parvati's underclothes
during love –
playful delicate hands fold across
two of his eyes
the third eye she kisses
may it protect you

– *anonymous*

Sattasai 5.55

NOTE ON THE *SATTASAI* OF KING HALA

King Hala appears by best estimates to have lived about 200 C.E. He was a ruler of the Satavahana Dynasty, but aside from his anthology, simply called *Sattasai*, or Seven Hundred Poems, he has left no record. At the outset Hala makes it clear his collection will focus on love poems, and he regarded poets as those people whose business it was to know love – know it in its intricate details – a position stated in much stronger terms in the *Kama Sutra*. The Satavahana is the same dynasty that painted the eloquent and infinitely tender Buddhist murals on the cave walls at Ajanta, yet Hala's anthology is resolutely secular. Two hundred and sixty-five poets appear by name in Hala's anthology, of whom eight are women. Forty of the poems are Hala's own and many more he probably arranged or even put into final shape. That hundreds of the poems go uncredited, including all of the final two hundred, raises a number of questions. Are they Hala's? Could women have written them, possibly courtesans at Hala's court? Were they uncredited folksongs gathered in rural villages and written down in verse-form by a capable poet? Part of their charm is that very likely we'll never know.

Four Arvanit Poems

Translated from the Arvanitika

I will burn your loom

I will burn your loom
As you have burnt my heart
I passed your house yesterday
I passed your house this morning
You did not stop weaving
You passed and repassed the shuttle
And blackened my day
Do not strike the threads with such hatred
I am not the vampire of your streets.

In Prison

How does the girl pass the day?
Zip and zap throwing the weaving shuttle.
When she goes to her loom
she is entering a prison.
Come, leave your loom,
It has torn your face.
I will become a black snake
and pass her the carding-comb through
I will become a white snake
and pass the threads for her
I will become a spotted snake
and pass the shuttle through.

A Dirge

Why is the mountain weeping?
The girl has died
The girl with blond hair
The girl with red cheeks
Her wretched mother, her wretched aunt
What can they say ... they weep and weep
They will drown themselves in the waters of the sea.

A Death Poem

Where are you going, sweet fragrance?
You slammed the door shut behind you.
Where are you going, sweet fragrance?
Do you not love your parents, do you not love your house?
Where are you going, lily blossom?
Do you not love your parents, do you not love your house?
Why should your raven eyebrows
be devoured by the earth?

The Arvanites are an ethnic minority living in isolated communities throughout Greece. They speak Arvanitika, an unwritten language which developed from Medieval Albanian. Their centuries-long isolation in Greece gave rise to a unique oral literature untouched by Modern Greek and Albanian literary trends.

Translated by Peter Constantine

Nuala Ní Dhomhnaill

Clingeann na Cloig

Clingeann na cloig rabhaidh ar na báid
solais atá ar ancaire sa chuan
faid a shiúlaimid neafaiseach go leor amach an cé
ag ithe uachtair reoite i lár an lae.

Siúlaímid lasmuigh den dtonnchosc cé go bhfuil stoirm
á bagairt is caipíní bána ar fhormhór na dtonn.
Tá suathadh maith ins an uisce is trasna an chuain
Binn Éadair ag craitheadh a chinn go magúil os a chionn.

I bhfad uainn ag íor na spéire tá long trí chrann,
rud neamhgnách go maith. Deirimse gurb é Manannán
atá ag marcaíocht a chapaill thar mhachairí bláfara a ríochta
is nach fada go dtiocfaidh sé suas chugainn is fiafróidh
an bhfeacamair aon rian
des na muca mara a goideadh inné uaidh ag aonach sa Bhreasaíl.

Gáirimid beirt. Aithnímid go maith an scór –
ár samhlaíocht ag dul de hop, scip, cosabacóid
thar spéir na hearraíochta, thar an ngnáthúlacht laethúil.
Tá an draíocht os comhair ár súl míle uair

sa ló. Anois féin laistiar dúinn tá spící na sáipéal
ag síneadh i dtreo na spéire le gach scalladh ón ngréin.
Tí Halla an Bhaile ag aibhliú faoina aolchloch liathbhán
is na tithe lóistín ag spréacharnaigh faoina ndathanna milseán

Leagann an radharc amach mé. Leagann fós
an spréach ghorm a lasann i ndoimhneas do dhá shúl mhór.
Tugann mo chroí aon phreab bheag éidreorach amháin
faid a chlingeann na cloig rabhaidh ar na báid.

The Warning Bells Ring

The warning bells ring on the lightships
at anchor in the harbour
As we walk, casually enough, out along the pier
eating icecream in the middle of the day.

We walk beyond the breakwater, although a storm
threatens, and most of the waves are white-capped.
There's a good roil in the water, and across the bay
The Hill of Howth shakes its high head in derision.

Far away from us on the horizon there's a three-masted ship,
A pretty unusual sight. I say it's Manannán,
riding his horse over the flowering plains of his kingdom,
and before long he'll come up to us and inquire,
did we see any trace
of the porpoises stolen from him yesterday at the fair in Hy Brasil?

We both laugh. We know the score –
our imagination going with a hop, skip and a jump
beyond the material orbit, beyond the daily commonplace.
Enchantment is right in front of our eyes a thousand times

Each day. Even right now behind us, the church steeples
stretch closer to the sky with each blast from the sun
The Town Hall shimmers in its pale grey limestone
and the guesthouses glisten in their candy colours.

It floors me. As does
the blue flame that lights in the depths of your large eyes.
My heart leaps just once, adrift
as the warning bells ring on the ships.

Translated by Kaarina Hollo

INTERVIEWS

NUALA NÍ DHOMNAILL

KAARINA HOLLO

MARIO RELICH

IAIN CRICHTON SMITH

Acts of Translation

AN INTERVIEW WITH NUALA NÍ DHOMHNAILL

Kaarina Hollo

*The poet and translator Anselm Hollo has said 'catching the tone of poetry written in a foreign language is an important part of the interpretive task, and it requires a sophisticated passive knowledge of that language: by 'passive' I mean an understanding of the language and culture (in the particular time and place of the work in question) not (necessarily) any kind of active fluency in it, (*Postmodern Poetry*, 43). You have worked with a wide range of translators, with varying degrees of mastery of Irish. How important do you think it is for a translator to have a mastery of the subject language?*

Rather than active mastery of subject language in every form and shape, I think that how Hollo puts it is the best way; a sophisticated *passive* knowledge of the language. Even Paul Muldoon, who for God's sake, has an honours degree in Irish, won't actually speak it to me. His excuse is that we have different dialects, but actually I think what happened, is that we were talking English when we first met, and that as most of our conversations go on in the presence of people (like his wife, for instance) who have no knowledge of Irish, we have continued in same. Paul, on the other hand, is immensely erudite about Irish. I still remember an impromptu peroration on the 'Fir Bolg', that he launched into once during a walk in the country when I just mentioned casually that the townland that we were passing through was called 'Cathair Boilg'. Of course, he was taught Irish in Armagh College by the great teacher and musicologist Seán Ó Baoill, so that explains a lot.

I think that Hollo's choice of the word 'passive' is important. More than anything else a certain humility in respect to the subject text is important. Some poets – we're talking of male, Irish here – lack that humility and think that they have much better Irish than they actually have ... Paul on the other hand – probably because he really has very good Irish – is most undefensive. When I faxed him the poem that was to be in *Poetry Chicago*, he rang back and asked questions like 'Who are these cows with the long horns'? 'Oh, that's a *seanfhocal* "bionn adharca fada ar na buaibh thar lear"' 'We don't have that *seanfhocal* in the North' 'Well, I'm glad to hear that you don't have everything in the North' – that kind of give and take, which I love, and which is genuine and loving. But he's the only one I've ever had that level of undefensive interaction with. Mostly I just send them the crib with the original (usually at their request) and then later on they send me back the finished translation.

How closely do you work with your translators? Does the degree of communication or collaboration vary?

I really haven't had the chance to work half as closely with my translators as I would have liked to. Mostly this is for temperamental reasons; poets (male, Irish mostly) are a notoriously prickly bunch. Sometimes the reasons have been geographical: Paul Muldoon for instance, is now in Princeton and recent translations have been accompanied by a flurry of faxes back and forward. Mostly the degree of collaboration is absolutely nil.

The only exception has been a recent week of collaborative translation into Turkish, under the aegis of *Annaghmakerrig* and *Poetry Ireland*. There I *had* to have a large input, as none of the Turkish translators had any Irish. I had to crib each line in the original, and say it aloud for them again and again. When they put anything in that was in the English translation alone I had to insist that it wasn't there in the original. I have reasonably good Turkish (though mostly, at this literary level, *passive*) and one of the main joys for me was the witnessing of the production of such wondrously complex agglutinative syntactical structures, sometimes of great beauty, that I could well appreciate as being the best way of doing the original, but could never have hoped to match the production of myself. We used to come out of each session drunk, and punch-drunk, from a kind of literary delirium. It was really marvellous. The results were impressive, too. My husband swears that the Turkish translations are much better than the English; and read so well you'd swear they were written in Turkish to begin with.

I would really love to work with translators in any of the other languages that I have a reasonable passive knowledge of; English, French, German, Dutch; but the occasion so far has never arisen. Redmond O'Hanlon's translations from Irish into French have been the only ones in which anyone has as much as deigned to ask my help. I'm working on it, though; as I would really like a good selection of poems in both French and German. Otherwise all this farting around to the 'Imaginaire' and the Frankfurt Book fair etc. will have been a complete waste of time.

How have the poems for your three bilingual collections been selected?

On a very 'ad hoc' basis, on the whole. For the *Rogha Dánta* Michael Hartnett, who had been commissioned by Raven Arts, came to me and said 'what poems do you want translated, Nuala?' and I went through my two books quickly and said 'this, this, and this'. I didn't put an awful lot of thought into it, I must admit and we both left the actual ordering of the poems in the book to Dermot Bolger. This, I can see now, created a lot of problems that I still haven't satisfactorily solved. For instance, 'Máthair' was translated without its *leathbhádóir* 'Athair', even though they were originally and deliberately published side by side in 'An Dealg Droighinn' as two sides of the same coin. I think that has been the main problem that is still mostly unredressed; that the poems were taken out of their original context, and now I'm not sure really how to put them back. One thing about Michael Hartnett, though; he did actually translate all the poems I asked him to.

The production of *Pharaoh's Daughter* was in some ways even more haphazard, in that I had, over a period of about ten years, accrued a reasonable amount of good translations which I used to carry around to readings on sundry bits and pieces of paper. Peter Fallon, who has an extraordinary nose for a good book, approached me and asked to take these various bits and pieces of paper off my hands, so that we might see what we had got. Then he commissioned some of the translators to do some more of them. The choice of translator for any particular poem I had cribbed was made by both Peter and myself. We sent them off a batch each, choosing poems that we thought might be up each poet's particular alley; – narrative poems in long lines for Ciaran Carson; 'demon lover' short lyrical stuff for Tom MacIntyre etc., but then a lot of the people only did a poem or two. Maybe they didn't like the stuff we had sent them. I never knew quite why, but a lot of poems that I would have liked to have got translated never really got done.

For *The Astrakhan Cloak* I cribbed the whole of *Feis* and it was sent off to Paul Muldoon. He rang me up and said 'That is an awful lot of poems, what do you want me to do with it?' I said 'Whatever else you do Paul, do the title poem, as I really need that for readings. Apart from that you can do whatever you like.' It is just as well that I specifically asked him to do 'Feis', as otherwise I don't think he might have; it is not really his type of thing; too rhapsodic and emotionally open, maybe. I know for a fact that he made very few changes in the 'crib' I gave him, as opposed to the more free-wheeling way he has made other poems his own. I was actually a bit surprised by his choice in the poems he translated. I know he seemed to emphasise the poems that had an 'otherworldly' dimension or intrusion. I dare say that they stuck out particularly with a kind of rarity value, given his present American background.

It had never even dawned on me that they were a particular 'theme' as such; as you know 'Feis' is almost already over-programmatically thematic in another way; but that was a method I had of somehow structuring what was a hell of a lot of various different kinds of poems. Otherwise 'an saol eile' is not such a big deal in Irish as it seems to be when it gets translated into English. I would even go so far as to suggest that in Irish it is quite common. Then again, this may be a projection of my own inner reality and may not be equally valid of other people's work. In retrospect, though, Paul was right to structure it thematically in a different way from the original, seeing that the whole book wasn't going to be translated.

*You have said that the translations of your work are 'only secondary manifestations, because the books in Irish have an architectonic structure of their own ...' (*Southern Review, *Summer 1995, 599-600).* Feis *(1991) is perhaps the most structured of your collections. Would you like to see that volume translated as a unified work?*

Yes, I would like to see it translated into other languages as a unified whole, but I accept at this stage that it is too late to do so in English. Instead the extra poems can be eventually mopped up as part of another volume of translations. But if I do ever get to work up the *Mermaid Poems* I am working on at the moment into a kind of extended series, or book within a book, then I think I will insist that they are published in English as a discrete entity, and in the same order as in the original.

*You have said 'that the translations are never more than a secondary consideration, and should not be taken to stand for, or to stand in for, the originals' (Krino, 14, 50) and 'my primary audience is those who read my work in Irish only' (*NYT *Book Review 8/01/95, 27). However, you have also pointed out that there is a 'disenfranchised audience, which would read me like the other if they had Irish. But they haven't, and it's not their fault they haven't Irish, not even here in Ireland. And that's where translation comes in.' (*Studies, *Aut. 94) What do you hope this disenfranchised audience gets from your work in translation?*

I feel I was very lucky that by the time I came out of secondary school I had a reasonably good literary facility in both official languages of this country. It meant I had a genuine choice when it came to using either as a literary medium. I think it is a real pity that every single citizen of this country is not given this as a *real* choice. It would seem to be their constitutional right, and the very fact that it is not a widespread situation makes me think of most Irish citizens as being seriously disenfranchised.

Mind you, what I *have* found is that there is a large audience out there who have a reasonably good level of Irish left over from their schooldays but who have never been in a situation since then where they have been able to practice the language or keep it up. No situational context, or contextual situation in which it might be a normal and natural thing to do. When they read the poems in a dual-language format they often start with the English versions but before long are looking over the page at the Irish, and before long again they are understanding much more than they ever thought they would. These are people who normally wouldn't dream of opening a book written in Irish; it would be a much too daunting prospect. I really think it is important to reach this audience. I know I have had countless people come up to me and say that my poems have sent them back to picking up Irish again, and that this gives me an unparalleled joy and pleasure. It is often the only thing that makes me get up in the morning and sit down to work. I find I feel very strongly about this, and the fact that for most of the people of Ireland – through no fault of their own – the whole fifteen hundred years of unbroken literary tradition in Irish is a closed shop really breaks my heart.

In a conversation with Medbh McGuckian published in the Summer 1995 issue of Southern Review, *you said that the most important thing in translation is 'to get the voltage that is behind the words.' Are there translations of your poems that you feel succeed particularly well in conveying that voltage?*

Well, quite a lot of the translations do that, but off the top of my head I'd say that the Muldoon translation of 'Mo Mháistir Dorcha' that was in the *Poetry Chicago* Irish issue, and which won us both the Bess Hokin prize, is my favourite at the moment. I said to him beforehand that I thought it might be impossible to put English on, as the particular four-line stanza with end-falling cadence has, to anyone who has heard Somhairle MacGill-Eain doing 'Hallaig' say, a particular fateful and fated quality, that could not possibly be carried by that stanza form in English. It is as near as you can get, I think, to a modern Irish/Gàidhlig classical metre. He knew immediately what I was going on about and got around the problem by using repetition and parallelism, almost in the archaic way it is used in 'The Psalm of Psalms' or in 'The Song of Inanna'. That really impressed me. I thought it was a marvellous way of getting the right 'voltage'.

I must say that Medbh McGuckian does that too in 'Geasa', and John Montague in 'The Broken Doll'. I know he gives the poem a more literary patina in English than it carries in Irish, but then from the beginning I saw it as a very pre-Raphaelite poem, and that is the quality that he gets across marvellously in English. For all that he has no Irish at all, Michael Longley gets that across too in 'Aubade', though he actually has told me that he thinks he improved on the original; tidied it up a bit, like. You can imagine the look on my face at that statement. He makes a much more Edwardian, dainty, Miss Tippy-Toes poem out of it; but given the prosodic registers of English, you would almost have to do something like this, to get the slightly over-written quality of the original across.

A poem that really is good on voltage is Montague's version of 'Blodewedd'; he gets the sound across very well, though I do think that the 'ladies toilet' bit at the end seems much more bathetic than it does in Irish. Again this is a clue to how very differently the two languages operate. Derek Mahon's version of 'An Rás' I like a lot too; it gets the hurried breathlessness of the original dead on.

Some of the translations in Selected poems/Rogha dánta *(1988) are your own. In an interview in* Innti *12 (1989) you expressed a fear that translating your own work might interfere with your composition in Irish: 'Raghadh prosóide an Bhéarla i bhfeidhm orm sa tslí ná beinn tar éis tamaill ach ag scríobh dánta Béarla i nGaeilge'. Do you still feel this way?*

The only reason at all that there are translations of my poems in my hand in *Rogha dánta* is that they were at hand since the time, way back in the early '80's, when I needed translations for the Poets' Tour of Scotland, and I didn't know any poet in English well enough to twist their arms to do the translations for me in time. I have never felt that I have developed, or have the need to develop, a poetic voice in English. I may be really wrong about this, and doing myself a bit of a disservice, as I do read a lot of poetry in English, and have worked up a bit of a prose style for discursive essays, etc. I still feel terrified about doing translations into English for the reason that you mentioned. It is like some sort of last barrier, a *cordon sanitaire* that keeps me sane, and genuinely bilingual, when so many of the surrounding stimuli arouse my English side only to action. 'Thitfeadh an dún deireannach le Seán Buí', or something like that, if I were to start doing translations of my own work. I'd be somehow ashamed to do it; my grandfather would turn in his grave ... it is a very deep, and maybe totally irrational fear and sense of shame; after all, Louis de Paor has done his own translations, and very successfully at that. Even 'cribs' I find very difficult – and at some ontological level quite pointless; after all, I've written the poem once, how can I possibly ever turn around and write it all again? Realistically, though, I know they help, and so I do them, but I don't presume to imply that they have any literary value whatsoever.

*Barra Ó Seaghdha has written that 'a writer in a minority language who is in regular contact with translators, who appears indeed to regard translation as an inherent part of the writing process, is running a risk. Subconsciously, and with no element of calculation, the degree of future translatability and the values of the English-language audience may become factors that penetrate and weaken the original impulse.' (*The Irish Review *14, 144) Could you comment on this? Do you feel that this is a risk actually facing Irish-language authors?*

I see Barra Ó Seaghdha's point, but the above process is part of my personal stratagem for dealing with it. I know for a fact that it works for me, and that there is no way that a calculation of future translatability bleeds into my actual writing process. On the contrary; I actually revel in the kind of traditional prosodic turns (like repetitions etc.) that most distinctly *do not* lead to easy translatability. If there is one thing that definitely gets up my nose it is the modern editorial slant in Irish of considering only as well-made a poem that answers to the dictates of English Literary Modernism. What I am always looking for, and seeking after, is something else entirely. I still don't know what it is, or if I will ever reach it, but every single poem is an attempt at embodying it.

In the conversation with Medbh McGuckian referred to above, you said 'The poets I feel I can learn from and appreciate on this island are you and Ciaran Carson and Paul Muldoon and Eiléan Ní Chuilleanáin.' Each of these poets has translated your work into English. Have you ever considered translating the work of these or any other poets into Irish yourself? Would you see any value in such an undertaking?

I have done some poems of Medbh's into Irish; some as a sort of 'thank you' for the ones she had done for me; others for the *Southern Review* piece you referred to earlier. If some sort of genuinely collaborative work were to evolve with other poets mentioned I might do them too, but I don't think it would happen otherwise; I don't really feel the ontological necessity; after all, everyone who has Irish has English too, and can read them in the originals.

The development of the language registers involved in producing poems in Irish which because they are translations of poems in English are very close to English poems, is something I am not only not interested in, but actually may highly disapprove of. Good English poems are translated into the kind of pseudo-Irish gibberish that gives the language a bad name, and the ready acceptance of which may actually do the language damage (I find in writing this that I have stronger feelings on the subject than I had even begun to realize). Translation from a language other than English is a different matter; e.g. Máire Mhac an tSaoi's recent attempts at Rilke's *Duino Elegies*, as witnessed in the most recent issue of *Innti.*

Douglas Sealy, in his review of Pharaoh's Daughter, *argues that most of the translations are actually Lowellian 'imitations', where the original poem is used as a jumping off point rather than translated (*Irish Times, *8/12/90). What is your response to this? Do you believe that the distinction between translation, on the one hand, and version or imitation, on the other, is a valid one? André Lefevere's description of a version, as opposed to a translation, may be apposite here. In a version, he writes,*

> *the emphasis seems to lie on the shock value of words and images ... the version's communicative value is increased by the use of exotic words ... (and) by means of paraphrase ... colloquialisms are introduced to break the uniformity of style ... (*Translating Poetry, *76-77)*

He goes on to say that version writers often comment on the text they are 'translating', describe features from a different angle, and make explicit that which is implicit in the source text.

I haven't read Lefevre's book on translation, so I don't feel entirely at ease in answering this question. I do see what you mean by quoting the pieces of him that you do, but I feel that maybe if I had read the book myself, and could see these pieces in context, they might mean something else to me, or would be in more of a position to agree or disagree with them.

I feel that in any translation there are all kinds of accommodations and compromises and equivalent balances that are set up due to a variety of causes which may not only be purely literary in their genesis. Time, place, general *Weltanschauung* and even the translator's personality are some of the imponderables that have a place to play in this ...

Also, at some deep level, I think that all poetry is an act of translation anyway, from some deep pre-symbolic level of sound-patterning and an almost molecular level of meaning (Kristaeva's 'chora'), which is never more than imperfectly captured by words on a page. I am so constantly plagued by the seeming arbitrariness of so much that finally finds its way onto the page, and the compromises and accomodations necessary in even getting it that far, that I suppose it does cause me to have a pretty 'laissez-faire' attitude to subsequent translations of it. Mind you, I have always put my foot down when it was a question of absolute mistranslation, for all the good it ever did me!

Also, though quite as neurotic in my own way as the next person, I am not actually a control freak, especially when it comes to other people's behaviour, and am more inclined to observe people in action with amazement and astonishment than actually try to do anything about it. So here completely non-literary parameters of my personality come into play as well, and what can we do about them? I'll never forget my absolute astonishment when Paul Muldoon translated my 'Bean an Leasa' into 'a bright young thing'. That is not what I had in mind at all, but then to everyone their own obsession! and I was actually tickled pink that he could have got something else out of it. And why not?

Every act of translation is first of all an enormously careful act of reading, and you really have to give the reader his/her due, as well. Does it make it a better or a worse piece of art if they then get something out of it that the writer had not consciously intended? I'm inclined to look on a poem as a bit like non-representational art; somehow a wide enough generalization from the specific that everyone can come along and hang their own personal hang-ups on it. Given my extremely vivid awareness of how the whole shebang entails such an enormous act of translation to even get down on paper in the first place, you can see how I would tend to be inclusive, rather than exclusive, of variant readings. Life is so much bigger than what we know of it, so why not go with the flow ... everything anyway being at best an approximation. I may be very wrong in this approach, and might well do with coming up against some really cogent arguments to the contrary. If so, I would welcome them, as this is a very vital and important area of experience.

January 1997

To Hold the Darkness at Bay

A CONVERSATION WITH IAIN CRICHTON SMITH
TAYNUILT, SPRING 1998

Mario Relich

> When the Highlands loses its language, will there be a Highlands, said I, with my two coats, losing, perhaps, the two.
>
> ICS in 'Shall Gaelic Die?'

In the opening poem of Ends and Beginnings, *itself entitled 'Poetry', you begin with a striking, even surprising observation: 'Poetry has nothing to do with who we are./ It cannot be explained by biography'.*

Certainly in the past a lot of poetry that I've done has been what I would call 'inspirational'. It can be set off by seeing an old shoe, or an old tin, or walking along the road and seeing a cloud.

In that sense, I think poetry doesn't depend on autobiographical things. The autobiographical things can fill the poem, but where the poem comes from is a different question, and it's very hard to analyse really.

Yet you admire Robert Lowell's later poems, many of which are highly autobiographical. It seems to me that what he wanted to do in his confessional poetry, particularly Life Studies, *is to somehow get closer to feelings of pain and so on...*

I think a lot of Lowell's poems are feelings of pain. Feelings about religion, feelings about 'Red Indians', feelings about the Civil War, and also feelings about what is happening in the world today. So I think that he was trying to encapsulate in his poetry a great deal of personal pain. That's one of the things I like about Lowell, it's a very *nervy* kind of poetry.

The other thing is, I find lots of resemblances between myself and Lowell. One of them, of course, is his move from religion, from his early religion, and my own atheism. Also, the fact that he was brought up in a kind of area which was very puritanical, traditional and puritanical, like New England, and also again the fact that he had on numerous occasions breakdowns, as I had for myself one breakdown...

One of your finest novels, In the Middle of the Wood, *I find fascinating because it deals with the phenomenon of mental depression in such a clear and detached manner.*

It was written after I'd had this mental depression, I could remember very distinctly – I don't know whether this is strange or not – but I could remember very distinctly everything that happened to me during my depression. I had total recall, and some of the things were weird and funny in many ways.

I thought I would write this down in the form of a novel, but one which really set down practically everything that had happened to me, as it happened. None of it, as far as I can remember was invented.

My impression is that the character in the novel really suffers from overwork, combined with a kind of residual guilt. Sometimes, as a writer, you do feel this guilt that you are not really a part of ...

That's right. You're an outsider. I've always felt that myself as a writer, that I was an outsider. But the funny thing that happened after I'd had this nervous breakdown is that I became more able to communicate with people than I had been before. I learned a lot of different things; there were very strange happenings.

Looking back on it now, from one point of view there were a whole lot of comic incidents, but being inside was absolutely tragic. The darkness was phenomenally black.

That's what makes it such a powerful novel, it seems to me. You confront that darkness, but in such a way that you can see it objectively, as far as that can be done.

I wrote it a year after I'd left hospital, so that I was able to see it fairly objectively. Afterwards I could also see the funny side of it...

... I do find Lowell very compatible. And there was a period in my life, probably about the seventies, when I really loved Lowell's poetry. I still do, but not quite the same way I used to then. There's a wonderful verbal music, brilliance in his poems. I actually met him once in Edinburgh and I asked him for his autograph. I couldn't make it out at all, it was like a spider's scrawl, I've never seen anything like it!

So, he's been obviously a key influence.

Yes, if we go on to talk about verbal music, a lot of your poetry goes beyond the expression of personal feeling, to try to find, perhaps, some kind of consolation against a universe that seems to be meaningless, and cold...

Well yes, I think this is true. In any dogma that I study, I never find anything valuable in protecting us against the darkness which, I think, is inevitable. All we can do is to guard ourselves in as many ways as we can. I suppose one of the ways in which I do that is by writing poetry. It's a kind of magic thing, to hold the darkness at bay.

As for verbal music, you see I come from a Gaelic background, and I find music in poetry very important. I think with our turning to free verse in a lot of contemporary poetry, even Gaelic poetry now, we've certainly moved into new areas of experience, and new subject matter, but I think that we've lost part of the verbal music that used to be in poetry. The 16th century, Donne, Tennyson... all those people had verbal music. I sometimes wish that we had more of it, but I find that maybe it's impossible.

To press that point further – verbal music, even in poetry that's not necessarily lyric?

I suppose lyric would be the most obvious place to find verbal music. I know, for instance, that Sorley MacLean believed that the long poem was impossible. He went back to the Gaelic songs of the 16th and 17th centuries, so that one of the things which differentiates MacLean's work from other writers' is that there is a lot of music in his work.

Maybe some day we might be able to go back to this kind of verbal music. Certainly it would be found in the lyric. But even in *The Wasteland* you find some of this music, and certainly in Milton you find it in prolonged passages in *Paradise Lost*, which is certainly not a lyric. You find verbal music there, really the music of the organ, as they say.

You started writing poetry when very young?

Yes, I was writing poetry when I was about eleven. This was partly because I used to be ill when I was young. I used to suffer from bronchitis, so I was in bed a lot.

Again, going back to this verbal music, I found that when I was reading poetry in my early years I had to read it aloud because I couldn't make sense of it unless I did. It's very strange.

I still remember when I was in Aberdeen at University, one day walking past a cemetery I was reciting a passage from *Othello* aloud and nobody was around. The passage started off where Othello says to people: 'Put up your bright swords, or the dew will rust them'. And I thought there was something about Othello that was very mineral. The play is very mineral. It suited Aberdeen very well in some strange way.

Since you mention the word 'mineral', your long poem 'Orpheus and Eurydice', published in PN Review, *has a lot of mineral imagery.*

The story of Orpheus and Eurydice has always fascinated me. In fact, when I was in school in Stornoway I really loved Latin because I had a wonderful Latin teacher, Mr. Thrale...

He becomes Mr. Trill in your story Mr. Trill in Hades ...

Yes, he was a wonderful teacher, and the two main stories I loved were 'Orpheus and Eurydice' and also 'Dido and Aeneas', both of which I've used a lot.

The story of Orpheus and Eurydice is very mysterious. I think it a very mysterious kind of story. I think everybody really knows about it. The poet is supposed to look for his wife among the dead. And then he is told not to look back, and he does, and she disappears amongst the dead again. It's obviously got connotations with Lot's wife. Maybe that's the same kind of story.

Yes, it seems to be an archetypal story.

Obviously it's something mythical, about the poet, the archetypal poet. Whether the story is trying to say that, when something is dead, the poet must move on to new things I don't know. But maybe that's what it's saying. It's saying that one must not live amongst the dead, but move on to new ideas, new things.

There's a lot about minerals in it because, of course, Orpheus had to go into the underworld to try to persuade Pluto to let Eurydice go.

When you first started writing poetry, at the age of eleven as you said, did you question religious dogma at that time?

No, not as early as that...

So the poetry came first?

Oh, the poetry came first. I started very young. What I did then, and I suppose most young poets do that anyway, I would read lots of poets and really imitate them. I would write sonnets and other forms when I was quite young, to gain mastery over these, and could write metrically if I wanted to. Of course, a lot of my own work is metrical. I adopted free verse in later years.

I've noticed from reading your essays in Towards the Human *that although you're against any kind of religious dogma, your essential attitude towards human beings is that you're definitely against any kind of completely materialist way of ...*

... Oh yes! Well, yes! I suppose that might even be a paradox, that I should be an atheist and yet not be materialistic, not be totally materialistic....

... In *Consider the Lilies* I created a puritanical old woman who is quite unlikeable, and yet at the end becomes more likeable, so that the final message of the book is hope rather than despair. It was the idea that Christ was more or less saying that you must take no thought for the morrow. ... 'Consider the lilies, how they grow; they toil not, neither do they spin' ... The idea was that this Mrs. Scott, this dogmatic and in many ways unlikeable old woman, reaches a stage at the end where she takes no thought for the morrow. She leaves her dogmas behind her, becomes a human being, and becomes vulnerable. The background is the Highland Clearances, which I had already written about in a play in Gaelic. I wrote the book in eleven days, during the Easter holidays in 1968...

... Why I'm really against religious dogma is because I feel that there is no possible way in which one particular dogma can interpret the whole world. As time went on, and I saw more in my particular religion, my own isle and how dogmatic it was, I turned against it. And later on I turned against most forms of religion, really because of what was happening in the world, and because very often religion was at the bottom of it. It was at the bottom of a lot of violence.

On the other hand, it's very hard. I can't say that I see human beings as being simply material objects. It's very hard to reconcile the two.

I also get the impression that you're very uncomfortable with categorising human beings into classes.

Yes, I don't like that either. For us, brought up on Lewis, well there was no such thing as a class-system. I remember in the 1950s when there were all these plays by the Angry Young Men attacking the class-system, I didn't really know what they meant, because in Lewis we didn't have a class-system.

The only people in any particular village in Lewis who would be considered different, or maybe slightly superior to the rest of the population, would probably be the minister and the doctor. But even they were judged by how good they were at their jobs, rather than whether they were naturally superior to us. And in fact though we were very poor, many of us in Lewis, we didn't actually think of ourselves as poor, we didn't actually think of ourselves as being peasants, and that there were classes above us. I don't think we ever thought in that way at all, really.

Yet you do think of yourself as a double man, which implies a division within yourself, even if it's not one caused by class. I understand that English, for instance, was at first a kind of oppressive language for you.

Well, the thing was, we were forced to learn English when we went to school at the age of five. When we went to school we were speaking Gaelic and there we were, forced to learn English on the very first day. So therefore we had to learn all our other subjects in English. And Gaelic was never spoken inside the school at all, only in the playground in those days.

So you grew up, I suppose, a kind of 'double man', because you were speaking Gaelic in the home and then you were speaking English in the school; and you were reading English literature; and you were reading English history. You weren't really getting to know anything much about Gaelic history at all. So this continued as we went on.

When I'm writing in English, it might be that I am not using the whole of myself. Then again, it may be that writing in Gaelic only, I wouldn't be using the whole of myself either. So there is this split in, I think, the personalities of people who grew up in the islands, between English and Gaelic, and maybe between emotion and education. I think this comes out in a lot of the poetry that has been written for instance, by people like Derick Thomson.

It's a split that seems to emerge in one form or another among Scottish writers.

Yes, it's there between the Scots language and English as well.

I wonder if it actually pervades a lot of 20th century writers? ... You've said in the past that you find Nabokov too dilettantish, yet he too was a 'double man', one of the most celebrated in the 20th century, writing his early novels in his native Russian, and his later ones in English; to be more precise, American English.

Yes I do, I find him, if it's the word, over-glittery.

But is that not more his works written in English?

Oh I don't know his Russian work, but when I read his novels in English I find they give off an extraordinary glitter. I don't really read him a lot. But someone like Conrad [also writing as a non-native of the language], though his work is dense, and I think at times quite difficult, doesn't have that kind of glitter I find in Nabokov. I don't know whether this stylishness, this ornamentation was something that he got from writing in the Russian. I don't really know. I find him dilettantish, I must admit. The way I would put it, I think he's a games-player, you know. There's something about him, using art in order to play a game. I don't really think of art in that way.

But he played the game brilliantly, within the narrow limits.

Oh yes ...

Yes, I'm sure it's true, that the double man split occurs, not just in Britain, but in other countries as well. Sometimes it appears, for instance, in the work of that Caribbean writer Derek Walcott, where he comments on whether or not he should still be speaking and writing maybe in some form of African language, rather than English, and he is surrounded by all this imperial heritage which he reacts against ...

And he is an islander as well...

He is an islander as well. This is the kind of thing that one does get. It's quite a common thing, but it creates all sorts of problems for the writers involved. You reach a stage where you don't know whether you should be writing in Gaelic or English. And then you think, well, should I decide to write, permanently, only in Gaelic; or alternatively should I decide to write, permanently, in English?

Sorley MacLean decided that his English writing, when he started off, was not authentic, so he decided to write only in Gaelic. Derick Thomson writes only in Gaelic. Donald MacAulay writes only in Gaelic. But I write in both English and Gaelic. In that sense, I suppose I am quite different from a lot of the other Gaelic writers, because most of them don't write in English. They write basically in Gaelic and sometimes, of course, they translate the Gaelic.

Then there's the interesting case of Scottish writers who deliberately adopt Gaelic, though they're not native Gaelic speakers.

That's right. There are some people who write in Gaelic, who have learned Gaelic...

Like Meg Bateman ...

Meg Bateman is one, and Christopher Whyte another.

What do you think about them?

I think these poets have done well. I suppose they introduce new ideas and new subject-matter into Gaelic. Yes, they've done very well. Really ...

I find Meg Bateman's case particularly interesting because she appears to feel that English is an alienating language.

Even though English is her first language...

For her, Gaelic seems to be a psychological need, or perhaps more accurately, a psychic need.

She has done wonderfully well. Her love poems in Gaelic are, I think, very very good.

Why do you *write in* both *languages?*

I think maybe because from the time when I was very, very young I was reading English books, when I was ill. In those days there were no children's books in Gaelic at all, and I got into the habit of reading books in English all the time. I was probably reading the same kind of books as a Scottish child who didn't know Gaelic, or an English child.

So it may be because of this penetration of my psyche at a very early age by English books. By reading so much, I became very interested in poetry by English writers rather than Gaelic writers.

So to double back again on the 'double man' dilemma, is it as if writers in the 20th century simply cannot be fully integrated into their societies?

I think you have to be extraordinarily lucky to be 'fully integrated'. I mean, Auden was always talking about people being lucky, and I think there is an element of luck in it.

I had, I suppose, a fair bit of difficulty as an English writer, because I was faced by two things: first of all, that the original language was Gaelic; and then, the second thing, this religion which was telling me that writing was itself vain, that artistic endeavour was vain. There seemed to be this kind of repetitive radio station inside me all the time saying that what you're doing is vain. This would come from the background of religion.

Was this a pressure on you?

It was to a certain extent, because I don't think I would ever make large claims for 'Art'. I couldn't go so far as Auden when he says that poetry changes nothing, but, on the other hand, I couldn't go as far as to say that 'Art will replace Religion'. Maybe that's because it's an inheritance from my own background.

What about Shelley's dictum: 'Poets are the unacknowledged legislators of the world'?

I don't think I would go as far as to say that. But again, that may be because of my background.

But can it not be argued, in fact, that to be a double man, as we've discussed, is enriching?

Yes, it can be argued ...

It can be seen in the work?

Yes, yes, I think that is possible. McLean himself says something about a divided intellect, so he found himself to be divided as well, I think. But as you say, it can be an energizing thing.

I suppose if you absolutely believed in any dogma, if you found yourself a totally committed Communist, you might be writing stuff ... or doing pictures that weren't terribly good. I think that actually happened with Communists, those people who were totally committed. Communists were writing books that weren't terribly good because there was no conflict. I think you probably do need conflict to write, or make good works of art. There must be a conflict within you.

What you say reminds me of the case of Brecht who apparently was a very committed Communist, but he also seems to have had an ironic stance towards Communism throughout his life.

Yes, he did. I wouldn't think of him as particularly dogmatic. The kind of people I'm thinking about are people like the ones who were attacking Solzhenitsyn in Russia. You know, who were apparatchiks, in a way. And yet they were still writing books, but books which made this ideology so important that there was actually no life in the characters, because there was nothing for them to attack, or be attacked by.

What do you think of Neruda?

Oh, I think he's a wonderful poet! I don't know how far he was a totally committed Communist.

Publicly, he seems to have been totally committed, but privately it might have been another matter?

I don't know. There are some wonderful things in Neruda. He had a tremendous compassion for the poor, which comes across strongly in his poetry...

... which perhaps over-rides his more dogmatic political attitudes?

I wouldn't imagine he allowed himself to be too dogmatic. I don't think any poet can really be a total dogmatist. I don't think a poet can follow a party line... or is able to follow a party line.

There must be an element of rebelliousness that comes out somehow or other. MacDiarmid is obviously a case in point. He was always rejecting the party line, then joining again when everybody else had left, and so on. I think politically involved poets, to be any good, must have this kind of rebelliousness.

Another 'double man', and in many ways a rebellious one, was Robert Burns. Let's go on to your poem The Human Face, *which is written in the Burns stanza. What does Burns mean to you?*

I think he is a wonderful writer of songs and lyrics, and a few great poems. What's the one about the elder again?

'Holy Willie's Prayer'?

Yes, 'Holy Willie's Prayer'. It's a wonderful poem, it's a great great poem by any standards. And also 'The Jolly Beggars'.

A lot of his poems I don't like.

I don't like the Burns cult, anyway, but he did stir me up when I was writing in the Burns stanza. The Burns stanza, though not very fashionable, allows you interesting and outrageous rhymes and it did test me to the maximum.

Also, of course, the poem itself is about a Burnsian idea. I've got as an epigraph: 'Man's inhumanity to man/Makes countless thousands mourn', so the poem is about man's inhumanity to man and is really an attack on dogma. I would say it's a very didactic poem, teaching a lesson, a full-scale attack on dogma down the ages. And it's also an attack on religion, it's saying that we don't need the kind of apparatus of angels, and all sorts of things that are spawned by a weird kind of spiritualism. We don't need any of that. All we need is the earth, and the earth should be enough for us.

It's a very long poem, sixty-four pages, so quite a long poem for me. I think it's a very unfashionable poem.

It's not quite a narrative poem, nor a satirical one, but it has philosophical links...

It's something I had to get out of my system. There is a certain amount of anger in the poem. I think there is genuine anger in the poem...

... which gives it its energy. In fact, Burns himself was often energized by anger.

Oh yes, there were times when Burns was very angry.

But The Human Face *seems to me also very much a philosophical poem, indeed, philosophers and philosophical ideas are often prominent in your work.*

Probably the philosopher who made the most impact on me at a certain point in my life was Kierkegaard. He fascinated me because he seemed to be a brilliant intellect, yet at the same time a poet.

Reading his philosophy is almost like reading poetry, and it taught me a lot about the way that religion operates, that there are different categories of religious people. Also, I was moved by him, by his life, because he was a hunchback and children used to laugh at him. There was great deal of pathos about this figure in Denmark. He had an absolutely brilliant mind in a crooked body, but what attracted me to him in the first place is that I saw the poet in him as well as the rigorous intelligence.

'Shall Gaelic Die?', which you originally wrote in Gaelic, is a poem structured like Wittgenstein's aphorisms in the Tractatus. *The poem argues that language makes us, rather than the other way round. A very significant concept ...*

I think it was Wittgenstein, or some linguist, who said that when we are born we are projected into a language. I suppose different languages differ from each other in their structures and in the range of their vocabularies, and therefore language actually shapes what we can say and can't say.

I mean, for instance, Gaelic as you'd expect is very strong on sea terms and fishing terms, but it has not ever been strong at all on philosophy and artistic criticism. Therefore, we couldn't really discuss in Gaelic, I think only to a limited extent, philosophical ideas of the density of Wittgenstein's, and that is because the language was the language of a people who were not intellectually developed, or involved enough, in that particular way.

I suppose, according to the language we are projected into, so will the range of our horizon be.

Immanuel Kant appears in your recent play, Lazybed, *written for the Traverse Theatre. Why does the play make fun of him?*

Murdo, the main character in the play, uses Kant as an image of the type of philosophy local people wouldn't know anything about. The Kant in the play is a very impractical kind of person, but for Murdo he represents someone who had written about the universe, about the world, and who appeared to have made some sense of the world. He is at the same time slightly eccentric, which he probably was.

Kant was a bachelor, and Murdo is also a bachelor. At one point, Murdo says to him, 'How did you like being a bachelor, how did you get on being a bachelor, how could you bear being a bachelor?' And Kant says you have to have a consuming idea.

The only consuming idea, Murdo says he has, is that when his mother died, he learned a new breakfast, which was marmalade slices with porridge. But Kant says that cannot be considered a consuming idea!

The personification of Death in Lazybed *is particularly effective. That, of course, goes back to medieval drama...*

Exactly, yes, it's amazing the way things come into your head. I remember when I was in Cambridge, many many years ago, and they were doing one of these Mystery plays, perhaps *Everyman*. There was this character, like Death, who walked about on stilts. I suppose it must have come back into my mind.

But Death is very much a joker, a trickster ...

Yes, he's a kind of jester. And the other thing about him is that he actually hates his job. He says at one point he hates killing people, and he hates killing the children. He gets drunk because he can't stand what he's doing, so he and Murdo get drunk together ...

Death makes the audience confront mortality, something that must be faced, yet entertainingly, as part of the fun and games of the play ...

I think the play *is* comic, yet at the same time quite serious.

Death appears to represent the cruelty at the heart of the universe, which isn't intentional cruelty, it's just the way things are.

It's just the way things are. That's what torments Murdo, you see. The basic idea behind the play is, really, why do people get up in the morning when they see the world around them, how terrible it can be, and how cruel? What makes them get up in the morning?

Is he your alter-ego?

Oh I think he is. Looking at Murdo, lots of people would think he was eccentric and even quite mad. He is my 'alter-ego' in the sense that, by using Murdo, I can pass judgements in a way that I wouldn't be able so easily to pass as myself. I can attack certain things that go on, in a form different from writing a newspaper article. The other thing is, to do it humorously.

The Murdo stories were written over a number of years. They're also, I suppose, influenced a great deal by Monty Python, because that's the kind of humour I loved, that kind of surrealistic humour. I think the Murdo stories have elements of this surreal humour. Essentially the humour had to be strange because I don't like most Scottish humour, I don't like couthy Scottish humour. I'm not at all keen, for instance, on Neil Munro's *Para Handy*. Lots of Scottish comedians I don't like either.

How about Ivor Cutler?

Oh yes, I like him. I like humour which is really weird, and makes strange jumps. It's a bit like my poetry. I like to jump from one image to another in my poetry. Similarly, in the Murdo stories, I like to make him jump from one point to another in a way which isn't at all obvious.

Murdo, it seem to me, originates very much from your experience of village life. In fact, there's a kind of paradox in the way you have described life in Lewis. It's very communal, but every person is given worth as well.

Oh yes, it was very communal.

It's just that everyone was respected, as far as I can see, in a way that perhaps they aren't in big cities, where if you don't have enough money ...

Oh yes, I mean there wasn't this idea ... at least I never felt it, that because someone in our village was poorer than someone else they were demeaned in any way by this. People in our village, I think, though the whole existence was to a great extent communal, people had their own individuality, their own particularities as well. But certainly it was a good place to grow up in, because it gave you a feeling of security. On the other hand, it also meant that there was this 'eye' watching you all the time. You were always aware of this 'eye' watching you. And I remember when I went to Aberdeen, leaving Lewis for the first time at the age of seventeen to go to university, I felt absolutely free. I felt free because I no longer felt that this 'eye' was watching me, watching what I was going to be like, and knowing about my father, my mother, knowing about my aunts, and knowing about us ...

Was there a danger of people categorizing you too much?

Yes, you just felt that they knew you, knew all about you. And if you weren't practical, as I wasn't, that they would know I wasn't practical. And then you made all your mistakes in this sort of glare from the village. Whereas if you were brought up in a city this wouldn't happen to the same extent. So you're more open to being judged, I think, in a village. At the same time, even though you were more open to being judged, your individuality was still, to a great extent, respected.

Iain Crichton Smith, thank you.

ESSAYS

STUART HOOD

CARLA SASSI

PETER McCAREY

Pasolini & Fruilano

Stuart Hood

ONE OF MY FIRST lessons in Italian linguistics took place in the fertile plain near Parma a few days after the Italian armistice on 8th September 1943. An escaped prisoner of war, I had taken the risk of speaking to a peasant in the fields in what I knew to be reasonably good Italian. He listened to me politely and then said in dialect: 'Here we do not speak Italian.' What he spoke was one of the dialects of Rome's Cisalpine Gaul – a territory defined by the Alps in the north and in the south by the ridge of the Appennines running from east to west. Through the centuries these mountains have been the frontiers of a linguistic region. In the far north of this region is Friuli, which borders with the Slav territories. Friulano, the language spoken there, was described by Gianfranco Contini, the eminent Romance philologist, who played an important part in Pasolini's life, as 'one of these languages which I do not know whether to call quasi-languages or minor languages'. Whatever its precise status it is closely related to Ladino, the language which is spoken and officially recognised in the Dolomites further west – a language to which, it has been suggested, Friulano bears the same relationship as Provençal to Catalan. It was in Friulano that Pasolini wrote his first published poems.

The political history of Italy with its multiplicity of separate states and territories gave Italian dialects strong roots. These separate entities were to be finally united in one nation – constitutionally at least – only when Rome became the Italian capital in 1871. Whether that unification was ever fully recognised is still doubtful. It is true that with the mass internal migration of the Fifties, when the peasants left the land and there was a simultaneous population shift from south to north, it appeared that the process of unification was being consummated. But as recent events have shown unity is still a political issue – particularly in Northern Italy. It is a political current that has cultural manifestations as was brought home to me in 1990 at a literary dinner in Brescia, one of the foci of separatist politics. Here my fellow guests – architects, surgeons, lawyers – spoke normally and unaffectedly in dialect. Writing in 1957 Pasolini said that Italy was a state without a linguistic tradition. The unification had given rise to a lingua franca – Italian, which was the common language, the *koiné* of the bourgeoisie and the bureaucracy of united Italy. It was also the language of practical relations between the various regions and the language of the press. (He would later add – of television.) This was the Italian my peasant did not speak. His dialect ranked below it and, by definition, below a third important category – the language of the literary élites.

Pasolini was born in 1922, the year that Mussolini came to power. He therefore received his education and cultural formation under a regime which disapproved of linguistic diversity because it ran counter to the Fascist doctrine of the strong state and strong central government. It followed from this that one possible expression of anti-Fascism lay in a writer's choice of language. Alberto Moravia once explained to me that his bare, neutral style was a deliberate political act – a rejection of the rhetoric, of the rotundity of much Italian writing, which found its most grotesque expression in the oratory of the Duce and his sycophantic press. In the same way poets like Ungaretti, Montale and Quasimodo, through the hermeticism of their poetry with its restrained enigmatic style, signalled their fastidious opposition to Fascist rhetoric. It was therefore an act of some political courage for Pasolini to publish in 1942 – just before the collapse of the regime – a small volume of poetry in the Friulian dialect entitled *Poesie a Casarsa* – Casarsa being a small town in Friuli. One of the three hundred numbered copies of the limited edition was sent by its Bolognese publisher to Gianfranco Contini, who was teaching at a Swiss University. Contini liked it very much and at once sent a review to *Il Primato* wondering 'if they will have it.' He was right to have doubts. *Il Primato* had been founded by Bottai, a prominent Fascist – a *frondiste* who had certain differences of opinion with Mussolini and in his review published not only dissident views but even some contributions by anti-Fascists. But *Poesie a Casarsa* proved unacceptable to him and the review had to be published in a Swiss Italian-language paper because as Contini wrote 'the censorship was watching carefully to see that no one said too much good of anything written in dialect.' This rejection was experienced by Pasolini as a personal insult and fed what a friend described as his 'visceral and cultural anti-Fascism.'

Casarsa in the province of Udine was the home of a peasant clan which could be traced back to the 15th century and from which Pasolini's mother was descended. Pasolini knew Casarsa as a child and continued to spend his holidays there. In the early years of the war he moved to Casarsa and settled in a village nearby. From an early age therefore he had been used to hearing all around him in the countryside Friulano, the language of the peasantry; but he did not speak it. What he did speak was Veneto, the provincial dialect used by the townspeople of Casarsa. So he was bilingual. At home however, his authoritarian father – an army officer and a loyal Fascist – allowed only 'Italian' to be spoken. Friulano had a literary tradition that went back to the 16th century but was a tradition that Pasolini dismissed as based on the language and culture of the petty bourgeoisie of Udine, the provincial capital. The Friulano with which he was familiar was different. It was spoken in a linguistic pocket, 'this side of the river' – the river being the Tagliamento, which runs down from the Alps through Friuli to the Adriatic. This was a language that was purely oral. It was pristine, belonged – as it were – to a linguistic Eden. For Pasolini it was at one with the smell of the smoke on the peasant hearths, of the flowers along the ditches and the sun-dried reeds. It had never been written down. Yet it had its own traditional poetry in the form of the *villota* – a quatrain with some of the qualities of the *haiku*. Some of Pasolini's earliest poetry in Friulano is in the form of the *villota*.

That his linguistic situation was paradoxical he understood very clearly. He found himself, he wrote, in the presence of a language from which he was separate: a language that was not his, one that was maternal but not his own, one spoken by those whom he loved with tenderness and violence, confusedly and candidly. His regression from one language to another – to one that was earlier and infinitely more pure – was a regression along the stages of existence. It was the only means available to him to return to the origins of his sensuality – and his homosexuality – which were otherwise barred. He could reach them only by regressing to a period of happiness that 'coincided with the charming landscapes of Casarsa', with country life. To him Friulano was 'a pure tongue of poetry' that led him, he recognised, close to 'more dangerous literary regions – e.g. Mallarmé.'

Pasolini had gathered round him in Casarsa a group of friends – several of them evacuees from the bombing of towns and cities of Northern Italy while others were young boys from the neighbourhood. This group constituted what he called a *félibrige* – after the literary movement started in Provence by Mistral in the 1850's to foster the Provençal language. Early in 1945 they founded the Little Academy of the Friulian Language. It aimed to foster writing in Friulano, to use the language to produce poetry that was aware of modern trends, and at the same time to combat the provincialism of cultural life in Udine which, with 'its meagre and backward group of literary figures,' could not 'boast of being culturally an outpost of the avant-garde.' In politics Pasolini had a similar stance. He was in favour of administrative autonomy for the province of Udine but opposed to the backward looking sentiments, the nostalgia, that inspired it. In 1948 he joined the Communist Party. His life among the peasantry, his close relationships with young peasants, his researches into their language, had brought him face to face with the social realities of their life. The result was a hatred of the bourgeoisie. It was the bourgeois provincialism of Udine that would lead to his being forced in 1950 to leave Casarsa, denounced by both the Christian Democrat politicians and the Communist Party for his homosexuality.

Clearly Pasolini's engagement with Friulano was in part inspired by his need to come to terms with his adolescence and sex. As he wrote, 'I had used dialect for subjective reasons, as a purely poetic language'. But his interest in language has to be set in a wider perspective than that of his psychological development. During the war and the Resistance, in which several of them had been involved, several Italian writers confronted the problem of finding a language in which to describe their experiences – the dangers and hardships they had shared with comrades who did not speak 'Italian'. Pasolini defined this as the search for a national-popular language. One solution was to develop the literary tradition of *verismo* which Giovanni Verga had established in the previous century, introducing into his writing the intonations and vocabulary of Sicilian peasant life. In the immediate postwar years this was the solution adopted by Cesare Pavese, whose remarkable novel about the Resistance, *The Moon and the Bonfire* has strong Piedmontese cadences. Pasolini saw himself as working in the same tradition in 1950 when he was writing *A Dream of Something*, a novel dealing with the fortunes of young men from Friuli as they adapt to postwar life and the crumbling of lofty political hopes. It was, he wrote 'a strange cross ... between Proust and Verga'. Pasolini was by then living in Rome and becoming immersed in the culture of the *borgate*, the working class estates and shanty towns on the outskirts of Rome whose inhabitants were immigrants from Southern and Central Italy, together with working class Romans displaced by Fascism's rebuilding of the capital city. This Pasolini began to learn from the boys with whom he had relationships that ranged from those of friendship to love. They were, he said, his living dictionaries from whom he learned a new language – the urban dialect that had developed in those grim settlements with their poverty and criminality.

Once again his emotional life, his politics and his literary activities were intertwined. Just as he had decided to make a literary medium of Friulano, which had never before been used in writing, so now he decided to give an aesthetic dimension to the dialect of the *borgate*. In this he was probably influenced by the Roman novelist, Carlo Emilio Gadda, who now became a friend. One of the most innovative experimental writers of post-war Italy, Gadda used a macaronic mixture of the Italian of the élites and Roman dialect in his remarkable novel *Quer pasticciaccio brutto de via Merulana (That nasty business in via Merulana).* When he arrived in Rome, Pasolini began to use the dialect of the Roman sub-proletariat in an objective way so as to obtain 'the most exact description possible of the world I had before me'. The result of this effort is to be seen in *I ragazzi di vita* which was written in the demotic speech of the borgate and published with a glossary for its readers. It caused an immediate scandal. It was scandalous in its use of language that was, in both senses of the word, 'vulgar.' Worse still it described a way of life that denied the claims of the Christian Democratic government, which had come to power thanks to US funding, to have solved Italy's social crisis – to have provided an alternative to the aspirations towards social justice which had inspired the Resistance. Segni, the Christian Democrat prime minister, who attempted to impose a right wing Catholic censorship, had the book submitted to the public prosecutor in Milan where the book was published, on the grounds that 'the work is found to be of a pornographic nature.' In the trial that followed eminent figures from Italian literary life appeared as witnesses for the defence. Pasolini was acquitted. Over the next few years he was to be charged frequently with various offences including blasphemy – but these cases arose not from his writing but from his work with film which he defined as 'the written language of reality.'

Pasolini's most important writings on the problematics of language are contained in a collection of essays collected under the title of *Passione e Ideologia*. In reading and reflecting on them I have been reminded of two things. One is the degree to which writers of my generation and background inhabited – as Pasolini did – a culture he defined as bilinguism. That is to say at school and with the children in my street I spoke Scots; but at home English was the only acceptable tongue although a Scots word might be used if it was – as it were – in inverted commas. I had friends however who habitually spoke only Scots at home. The other is the similarity between some of his arguments and those deployed in the debates in the Thirties over the use of Lallans – debates in which, as students, we were deeply involved. There is a clear parallel to be found between Pasolini's work with Friulano and MacDiarmid's assertion that Scots was a language suited for a wide range of poetry and his support for the view that 'a poet can do what he pleases with language if he can fit it to his purpose.' Like Pasolini he refers back explicitly to Mistral's *Félibrige* and quotes him as saying that 'A language is like the shaft of a mine' for at the bottom of it there have been deposited all the fears, all the feelings, all the thoughts of generations.' Pasolini's criticism of the provincial literary tradition of Udine have their counterpart in MacDiarmid's scathing attacks on the 'Burns' nicht' tradition and on the sentimentality which marked so much poetry in Scots from the nostalgic Jacobitism of Edinburgh ladies to the émigré wistfulness of Charles Murray's *Hamewith*. His introduction to the *Golden Treasury of Scottish Poetry (1940)* – apart from being an instalment in his long feud with Edwin Muir over the literary validity of Scots – is a manifesto in support of poets who wrote in a Scots 'which is a synthesis of all the dialects into which Scots has degenerated and of elements of Scots vocabulary drawn from all periods of our history.' His list of poets writing in Scots includes William Soutar, Marion Angus and Helen Cruickshank (to whom he might have added Violet Jacob). Of those, only William Soutar would, from today's perspective, be seen as an important figure. The one poem by Helen Cruickshank included in the anthology is firmly rooted in rustic sentimentality. What he rightly stresses is the importance he and others – including Soutar – placed on bringing Scots verse into the main stream of European literature and with justice he cites his own translation – or imitation, to use Robert Lowell's term – of a great poem by Blok which is built in to *A Drunk Man Looks at the Thistle*. His *Water Music* is an avowed challenge to Joyce on his own ground of language.

MacDiarmid has to admit that Scots, at the time when he was writing, was used for few purposes save poetry. I can recall only one prose work by him in Scots – a short story in *The Modern Scot*. He mentions rather vaguely 'the improvement in the use of Scots in novels and plays' and might have cited the work of Lewis Grassic Gibbon. But for anything comparable to Pasolini's use of language in *I ragazzi di vita* we have had to wait for the work of James Kelman and Irvine Welsh and the establishment of demotic Scots as a literary language.

Bridging Identities

Translating Pasolini's Friulian poems

Carla Sassi

> '*Bon Diu, Diu amic, su lis alis da la nustra lenga provensàl, fa ch'i possi rivà ta lis ramis dai usiei*' P.P. Pasolini, translated from Frédéric Mistràl

> '*I want ti be as harsklike in my singin/As yon wee queyn ti me is whunstane hertit.../Gang, O my poem, gang strecht ti yon woman/That hes my hert sae woundit...*' Tom Scott, translated from Dante

THAT REGIONAL IDENTITY is always strong wherever one travels to in Italy is a fact that can hardly be regarded as surprising if one considers the young age of the Italian central state – born as late as 1861, at a time when the most powerful European central states had long been consolidated and were developing their respective Empires – as well as the distinct political and social history of the individual areas that compose it. Regional identities (and with them local dialects) have survived the limitations imposed by the centralising Fascist regime, and even the levelling influence of educational institutions and the media in the post-war period. Predictably, the issue of local identity is felt more urgently in those provinces which – for different reasons – have not had a leading role in the making of the Italian nation, either politically or economically: Friuli certainly belongs to this marginal and somehow 'less Italian' Italy, as Pasolini implicitly described it.[1]

A rural and fairly poor region until recently, which benefitted neither from the booming growth of the port of the neighbouring city of Trieste in the hey-day of the Austro-Hungarian Empire, nor from the affluence of the industrialised North-West in the 1950s and 1960s, Friuli remained distant from Italy even when it was eventually annexed in 1866.[2] Distance from the 'centre' – cultural, political, economic – was enhanced furthermore by language: Friuli distinguished itself linguistically from the Italian North-Eastern regions for the resilience of its ancient Romance language[3] (*Furlàn*), this being the only area where the Venetian dialect, which established itself in this part of the country in the course of four centuries of domination by the Republic of Venice, did not replace the local speech.

In a few cardinal traits and values – continuity with an ancient and dignified tradition, isolation and resilience – Friulians have for a long time proudly identified the most persistent signs of distinction of their culture. These were the very traits which attracted young Pasolini – educated in Bologna but son of a Friulian mother – and which were originally re-elaborated in his works. One of his numerous, outstanding achievements as a writer and as an intellectual is undoubtedly the 're-invention' of Friulian identity, as well as of its language and literature, in the twentieth century.

*

To be a Friulian meant for a long time to be outside History: at the margins of Italy, geographically as well as economically, Friuli remained largely unknown to most Italians, who would tend to identify it culturally and linguistically with the neighbouring Veneto. This 'silence' of course became more strikingly obvious in the Media Age: virtually no form of representation of our culture and language, either 'high' or 'low', either literary or popular, came from 'outside', to the point that it was quite common for national TV speakers to mispronounce the name of our region (['frju:lı] – *Friul* ['frju:l] in the local language – is a contracted form of *Forum Julii* 'Julius' market'). The idea of 'Friulianity' was at the same time very strong, rooted as it was in an ancient and dignified tradition, and very weak, insofar as it was largely described from a limited 'internal' perspective. Pasolini's revolutionary representation of Friuli broke this isolation, as well as the barriers of a provincial and anachronistically 'sentimental' literature, cultivated by middle-class literati. His vision combined the 'internal' perception of his Friulian childhood and adolescence (he used to spend his summer holidays in Casarsa – his mother's home town – and settled here with his family from the War years to 1950), with the 'external' perspective of the scholar of humanities, who had studied at the University of Bologna under the guidance of some of the most distinguished and eminent Italian scholars of the time (Gianfranco Contini was one of them). For the first time Friulian language was dragged out of geographical and literary marginality into a European (Romance) context. In this sense, to this day, Pasolini's Friulian works represent a formidable corpus of texts which 'tell' the land, the people and the language in a way that is still unrivalled. These works include several essays on Friulian language, culture and politics appeared on various Journals and newspapers,[4] a series of poems in Friulian (collected in *La Nuova Gioventù. Poesie friulane 1941-1974)* and a novel in Italian, *Il sogno di una cosa*, written between 1948 and 1949 and published in 1962, which offers a piercingly beautiful portrait of the life in the villages around Casarsa, as seen through the eyes of three young boys, bound by the same passion for politics and for life – while two of them are also deeply linked by an untold and unrealised bond of love. Pasolini also wrote a play in Friulian, *I turcs tal Friúl,* published posthumously in 1976,[5] and justly described as a great 'peasant epic': the play is set on the 30th of September, 1499 in Casarsa – at the time when Turks had invaded Friuli and were plundering and setting fire to the villages, slaughtering their inhabitants – and builds on the tragic wake of the villagers, who gather in the main square to pray and wait for the accomplishment of Fate...

At the time when Pasolini shifted his attention on Friulian language and culture, Friuli was basically a peasant society: Udine, its middle-class 'capital', would either despise it or look at it in sentimental, 'kailyardic' fashion: no one had tried – or had been up to the task – in the course of the nineteenth and the twentieth century to develop its ancient folk tradition into a modern, European tradition. The best things which had been written in that language – according to Pasolini – beside the *vilotis* (popular folk-songs), were confined to a restricted number of vernacular writers for whom he showed limited appreciation. Certainly – for the reasons aforesaid – Friuli's strongest sense of cohesion and distinction was to be found in its language: a Romance language, as the Gorizia-born linguist G.I. Ascoli classified it in his *Saggi Ladini* in 1873 (that are to be regarded as the first scholarly investigation on Friulian), which therefore does not belong to the same 'family' as other Northern Italian dialects[6] – a theory espoused by Pasolini who proclaimed: 'Lingua ladina, dunque, non dialetto alpino',[7] thus contradicting the scholars who – as Carlo Battisti – had 'degraded' its status to that of an archaic Alpine dialect of Northern Italy. Language or dialect – if we can set aside the linguists' controversy on terminology for a moment – it is a fact that Friulian sounds 'foreign' even to the ears of the neighbouring Veneti, and that its 'obscurity' certainly has marked a borderline which has proved to be much stronger than any geographical or political division. No surprise then that language, and the language question, became the central issue in Pasolini's writings on Friuli, the axis around which his ideology and poetic vision revolves. Language and landscape appear indissolubly linked in Pasolini's writings: the best synthesis is offered perhaps in the description of his journey by train from Bologna to Casarsa, a journey conveyed in terms of changing landscape and language – the subtly alterating hues of the fields heralding the wild and rough beauty of the Tagliamento valley and the 'ghostly light blue' outline of the mountains of Carnia, seem to offer the traveller a perfectly matching correlative objective of the ancestral words of its language, words like *fuejs, aghis, mari*[8]... I have always thought it is no mere coincidence that Pasolini often chose to portray Friuli as its distinctive landscape features come slowly into focus, from behind the window of the train crossing the smooth plain of Northern Italy. Pasolini's 'Friulian period' in fact can be seen as a journey back – in time and space – to his maternal roots and to a prelapsarian state, as well as to a province where he could still cherish the 'smell of a Romanic land, of a marginal area... an alpine Italy with a neo-Latin flavour, still stupendously recent'[9]...

A group of writers and intellectuals – among whom Nico Naldini – joined Pasolini and founded the Academiuta ('little academy' in Friulian), a workshop proposing to discuss and develop the new status of Friulian as a literary language as well as to bring forward a new way of 'writing' the land and the people. The Academiuta advocated a revaluation of the folk tradition as well as a rejection of the mainline vernacular tradition which voiced a middle-class, sentimental idealisation of Friuli, kindling a lively debate that involved a long-established cultural institution as the Società Filologica Friulana (accused by Pasolini of being 'antiquated'[10]). Given this premise, it is not surprising that Pasolini chose to write, rather than in the literary standard sanctioned by the Società Filologica, in the variety spoken *di cà da l'aga,* that is in Western Friuli... The reasons which Pasolini gave for this choice can be effectively summed up in his own words: it is 'an ancient language and yet still virgin... in which common words can still suggest the original images',[11] an archaic and unrefined language, which had not been 'corrupted' yet by a literary tradition. This 'virginity' was obviously regarded as a great asset by someone who was aiming at writing a new literature, furthermore Friulian – even in its Casarsa variety – had the full the dignity of a *language*, and could therefore voice a poetry worthy of a 'national', modern tradition: a goal which dialect literature – in Pasolini's definition, 'delayed' (*ritardataria*) and sentimental – could never attain. The first and foremost test for the Friulian tradition was then to measure up with the great poets of the European tradition: the journals published by the Academiuta between 1944 and 1947 – as the *Stroligut di cà da l'aga*[22] – often presented, beside poems, short stories and essays on sundry topics (mainly literary and linguistic but also on politics), translations (or 'reconstructions', as they were termed) from major poets, such as Mistràl, Verlaine, Ungaretti... This represented the best evidence of the *language* status of Friulian: only a fully-fledged language could stand the confrontation with some of the most difficult Romance poets... Consistently with the idea of literary translation promoted by the Academiuta, 'reconstructions' stood by themselves, with no original version facing them – they were in all respects new poems with their own full autonomy and beauty.

The Academiuta members – like most Italian intellectuals at that time – seemed to privilege the Romance tradition to the detriment of 'Anglo-Saxon' literature: one may wonder how they would have reacted to the fact that in Scotland, just as in Catalunia, a contemporary generation of writers was facing and theorising a set of problems very much akin to theirs... Hood's essay justly points at the similarity between MacDiarmid's crusade on Scots as a literary language and Pasolini's project. Certainly other points in common can be found between Friulian and Scottish *félibres*: I think it would not be out of place to compare Pasolini to James Leslie Mitchell/Lewis Grassic Gibbon, as both writers chose to give voice to the oral tradition of an ancient, long-silenced peasant culture, thus resolving to start from a 'clean slate', rather than continuing along the established lines of a written, 'antiquated' tradition, and inventing a 'new' language for what they envisaged as a 'new' literature (respectively Casarsa dialect and North-Eastern Scots). Furthermore neither of them joined officially autonomistic movements, even though both showed interest and participated in the contemporary debate on nationalism/regionalism. Certainly, to stretch these comparisons any further would be unwise: what Pasolini might have thought of the writings of MacDiarmid and Gibbon can only be surmised on the grounds of his writings on the Provençal or the Catalunian poets...

The publication of Scott's and Hutchinson's translations – or rather 'reconstructions' – of Pasolini's Friulian poems can be regarded ideally as a delayed meeting between two groups of intellectuals who (like other representatives of minority cultures who were striving for recognition at that time in Europe) had certainly much in common. Our curiosity – how they would have evaluated each other's achievements – will remain unsatisfied: however, each of the 'reconstructions' published for the first time in this issue represents a valuable attempt at making up for the lost opportunity, and at throwing a bridge across time and cultures...

*

Tom Scott seemed certainly the ideal 'bridge-maker' in this context: a poet himself, as well as one of the most sensitive translators of European poetry into Scots (even though, regrettably, a collected edition of his translations has not seen the light yet), he also had a good knowledge of the Italian language and had already tried his hand – with considerable success – on difficult poets like Dante and Ungaretti. In September 1994 I sent him a copy of *La nuova gioventù* (which includes translations in Italian of the Friulian poems) and asked him to have a look at it, and think whether he might like to translate some of the poems. I offered my knowledge of the Friulian language as a support to his work. I received an almost immediate reply, together with a translation of the first two sections of 'Li letanis dal biel fí'[13] ('The litanies of the beautiful boy'). In his short letter Tom appeared to hesitate: '... It seems to me that a dialect poet would do better, not a literary Scots one like me. The Friuli would go fine in Aberdeenshire Doric, I think, by a native speaker of it...'.[14] I objected to that, claiming that while it was true that Pasolini's Friulian was based on a local variety, it also achieved the quality of a refined literary language. Furthermore I thought that his translation was beautiful. He accepted to carry on the job: his second and last translation was 'Il dí de la me muàrt'[15] ('The day of my death'). The degree of appropriation revealed in the translation of this poem is striking – themes such as the perception of approaching death, the sense of a 'post-lapsarian' state of failure and sterility must have deeply appealed to Scott, who had dealt with them previously – as in his 'Views from Myeloma' and 'The Paschal Candill'. Scott omitted the caption – a quotation from the Gospel (John, 12.24: 'Verily, verily, I say unto you, Except a corn of wheat fall into the ground and die, it abideth alone: but if it die, it bringeth forth much fruit'), which in Pasolini's poem connects with the two closing lines, and – interestingly – chose to keep the Italian title; there are also a few significant lexical and grammar adjustments in his translation which – I am sure – cannot be simply justified through purely aesthetic criteria, as when the 'sanctity' of the poet's heart becomes his 'sacrifice' (l. 25). The note accompanying his work this time was even more laconic: he said he felt tired *(sono stanco!* he wrote in Italian[16]), and expressed the wish to hear the original sound of the poems. I was planning to be in Edinburgh the following year, and rather than sending a recording of the poems straightaway, I put it off till then; I thought it would have been more pleasant and more fruitful for both of us to discuss the translations and to read out the poems together, as we had done in the past several times. Unfortunately, when I arrived in Edinburgh, in August 1995, Tom was already in hospital, and by the time I left he had passed away. It will be always my regret that he did not manage to listen to the original sound of the poems, as he had wished to, and that he had not time to 'recreate' more Scots versions of Pasolini's poems. The posthumous publication of his contribution is also an opportunity for me to pay a small tribute to a friend and a poet whom I greatly valued.

Sandy Hutchinson's contribution to the building of the 'bridge' is equally valuable and perfectly complementary: a sensitive and gifted translator, he approaches the poems from a different perspective, one that Scott had deliberately discarded. In fact Hutchinson resorts to a *local* variety of Scots, rather than the standard literary one adopted by Scott – the Buchan dialect. In Hutchinson's 'recreations' Friuli *is* Buchan and the appropriation of both language and landscape takes place in a way – I believe – Pasolini would have greatly appreciated – as in 'Furth an Awa', where the young boy becomes a 'Buckie loon' while the plain of Friuli magically merges with the 'Buckle braes'. The result is striking: the poems are endowed with a new sound and a new rhythm, and yet they are able to suggest Pasolini's Casarsa language in a way that Tom's poem cannot achieve. Sandy also worked on the Italian versions, and patiently coped with my pedantic comments and glosses... while on my part I wish to thank him for providing me with a full set of notes glossing – very accurately – the Buchan words, in a way that certainly made my *Scots Concise Dictionary* almost redundant. We had also time to discuss personally the poems, which certainly helped us in what appeared as a very complicated and challenging cross-cultural journey, involving four languages, as both the translators and myself at times had to resort to the mediation of Italian and English dictionaries. A very fruitful and enriching journey for all that, a journey which – it is certainly to be hoped – someone will resume, and perhaps carry further in the near future.

NOTES

1 In 'Il treno di Casarsa' in N. Naldini (1993), p.166 (orig. published in *FMR*, no.28, November 1948), Pasolini describes Brindisi, Napoli, Crotone, Palermo as 'l'Italia più Italia'.
2 The Eastern part of Friuli – the area around Gorizia – remained in fact under Austro-Hungarian rule until 1918.
3 The border-line dividing a 'language' and a 'dialect' is often thin and largely depending on political issues: in this context the use of the term language referred to Friulian seems largely justified not only by the definition of several linguists, but also by the existence of a literary standard and a grammatical norm, and the fact that both the Italian government and the EEC have included Friulian in the list of minority languages.

4 Collected in a volume edited by N. Naldini (1993). A recent anastatic edition of the journals of the Academiuta – also edited by N. Naldini (1994) is also available (see Bibliography). Naldini – a cousin and a close friend of Pasolini, as well as an active member of the Academiuta and a writer – has written possibly the most sensitive and enlightening essays on Pasolini's Friulian works.
5 The national premiere of the play was held within the Venice 'Biennale Teatro' on the 11th June 1995, staged by the Compagnia Teatridithalia – Elfo and Teatro Stabile del Friuli-Venezia Giulia, and directed by Elio De Capitani.
6 Similar investigations were carried out by T. Gartner at about the same time. The two scholars were in agreement in that our language enjoys a certain degree of autonomy within the group of the so-called 'Ladin' ('Rhaeto-Romanic' in Gartner's terminology) languages, spoken in the Grisons in Switzerland and in four Dolomite valleys near the Sella massif.
7 'Il Friuli autonomo', in N. Naldini (1993), p.256 (orig. published in *Quaderno romanzo*, June 1947).
8 'Leaves', 'waters', 'mother'...
9 'Il Friuli', in: N. Naldini (1993), p 189 (orig. broadcast on the radio by RAI – national channel – 8th April 1953). My translation.
10 Cfr. 'Tranquilla polemica sullo Zorutti', in N. Naldini (1993), pp.214-217 (orig. published in *Libertà,* 16th October 1946). It has to be stressed that the project of the Academiuta was mainly literary, and was not actively involved with other contemporary political movements aiming at Friulian autonomy, even though Pasolini dealt with the topic in some of his writings.
11 'Volontà poetica ed evoluzione della lingua', in: N. Naldini (1993), p. 207 (orig. published in *Il Stroligùt*, April 1946. My translation.
12 In Friulian *stroligut* is a popular almanac, while *di cà da l'aga* indicates the area of Casarsa, that is West of the Tagliamento (literally 'this side of the water', the 'water' being the Tagliamento, the main and widest river in Friuli, and therefore – metonymically – *l'aga*).
13 'La Meglio Gioventù (1941-43). Parte I', in: P.P. Pasolini (1975).
14 Letter to C. Sassi, 10.9.94.
15 'Seconda forma de La Meglio Gioventù (1974). Parte II', in: P.P. Pasolini (1975).
16 Letter to C. Sassi, 29.11.94.

BIBLIOGRAPHY

P.P. Pasolini (1942), *Poesie a Casarsa*, Bologna: Libreria Antiquaria Mario Landi
P.P. Pasolini (1954), *La meglio gioventù. Poesie friulane*, Firenze: Sansoni
P.P. Pasolini (1962), *Il sogno di una cosa*, Milano: Garzanti
P.P. Pasolini (1975), *La nuova gioventù*, Torino: Einaudi
P.P. Pasolini (1976), *I turcs tat Friúl*, Udine: Ed. rivista 'Forum Julii' (2nd ed. Udine: Società Filologica Friulana, 1995)

N. Naldini (ed), (1993) *Pier Paolo Pasolini. Un paese di temporali e di primule*, Parma Ugo Guanda
N. Naldini (ed), (1994) *Pier Paolo Pasolini. L'Academiuta friulana e le sue riviste*, Vicenza: Neri Pozza

Find an Angel and Pick a Fight

Peter McCarey

Animal, vegetable or mineral

A BIRD WAS footering about on the gravel of the roof below, and I was trying to make out what it was. Charcoal head shading to mid-grey body, white flashes on the wings, russet rump. Much of the time it was only visible in movement, when the parallel white lines showed up. And I wondered, knowing that the best method of camouflage breaks up the lines of the structure, why every bird and beast from the most ostentatious to the most sleekit has bilateral symmetry. And plants extend round a line, and minerals round a point. Mineral, vegetable, animal, growing from point, line, plane. Fixed, flexible, mobile: the stricter the symmetry, the freer the creature. Is there an order of symmetry above bilateral? or below spherical? And humans, with our moral codes and formality in art, are we looking for freedom in a higher symmetry? Could it be formulated for verse? That's my real question, because as usual I'm only interested in theory as raw material.

To be more precise, minerals in this world aren't spherical, unless you count the oblate spheroid itself. But there's the stars, and the planets. Other mineral states derive from them. Gravity, collusions and collisions make the fractures and structures of rocks and crystals here.

For the radial symmetry of plants I'm thinking of trees and their roots, of thistles, roses, clumps of gorse and grass. I know they can start with punctate seeds and end with superficial leaves, but the governing axis of symmetry is the line. Animals have symmetry about a plane, which is only pliant, into the reflex dimension, and when the muscles relax they straighten up (watch how fish swim); the line, though, can twist and loop into another two dimensions, so that even when they are bilateral, plants are never so straightforward: a leaf is mapped onto its mirror image, the pair rotates up a tendril helically, boughs bend and twigs twist out to the light. Ach, I should be writing this in winter. Theories work better then. As it is, spiricles are unfurling from under crumbs of earth, shaking out into crossed pairs of smooth and serrated leaves. There are hundreds of different options: spiral fern shoots, sycamore hands, and maple, where leaves are certainly bilateral but also, like side aisles, echoes of the centre, diminishing fractally into their own serrations. Corinthian sprouts from doric severity.

As to animal symmetry, I know about amoeba and protozoa, but take this heuristic: if it's too wee to stamp on, it doesn't count. Sea anemones may plant themselves on rocks, and starfish revert from bilateral to apparent radial symmetry, but they're not the only creatures that don't know what they're about. It's curious that animals, which are not particularly symmetrical inside, are quite symmetrical outside: animal limbs are congruent, and the colouring, to return to the start (it was a black redstart), is just about absolutely symmetrical. Why? There are compelling functional explanations of the symmetry of bodies that want to follow their nose – such as avoidance of walking in circles. But why bilateral symmetry of decoration? Pierre Aubry, after some head-scratching, came up with a counter example. The sole, which is born a flat, vertical fish, develops into a horizontal flatfish. One of its eyes migrates round the corner so it can have a better view of the ocean squashing it some more. This means that one of its sides has two eyes, the other none; one side is one colour, the other another. I checked this up at the fishmonger's, and in a way he's right: the sole's mouth is along one edge, like the zip on a toilet bag. Nevertheless, it's more than half-way towards achieving a new axis of symmetry of the traditional sort, along a line that runs at right angles to the shortest route between its eyes. Why?

Another species of flat fish: imagine a dozen nacreous hatchets with the features of Tam Dalziel (sorry, Tam). If you can't, then get to Basel Zoo and look at the creatures tacking round over the label Selene vomer. They're called St Pierre or John Dory when they hit the fishmonger's slab, by which time they look more like Douglas Hurd. (Wrong again: John Dory is Zeus faber. But anyway ...) These creatures are symmetrical and identical: specimens of their species. This lump of clay has no symmetry. This human face has surpassed symmetry. A specimen abstracted from the species is symmetrical, but the unrepeatable individual steals from symmetry. Rubato. My symmetry says I am, and my mark on it says I'm only here the once. How does it go? asymmetry, symmetry, dissymmetry, then either dissolution or higher order symmetry? Maybe.

Groups of symmetry

Space/Time	Wave/Particle	Rhythm
Point	Mineral	Logic
Line	Vegetable	Rhyme
Plane	Animal	Metaphor
Body	Human	Naming

Each successive group incorporates the previous one – geometrically in column 1, physically in column 2, and literally in column 3: metaphor can entertain logic, for example, whereas logic, with the law of non-contradiction, cannot accommodate metaphor.

I have extended the 'animal, vegetable and mineral' categories by one at either end: subatomic, which I don't understand, and human, which I haven't really grasped either. In the nineteenth century there would have been a 'superhuman' category, courtesy of Solovyov or Nietzsche, but that hubris has nearly lost us our human specificity. 'God is dead' led to 'I is dead'. I don't think poetry can touch the godhead. It's only human. But human it is.

It would seem that Big-Bang archaeologists are projecting a golden age of supersymmetry in ten dimensions or so. People like John Ellis try to reassemble the Ur-version, rather as classicists infer Orphic cosmology from slighting references in Aristotle, or the way theologians chase through Coptic and Armenian translations for something nearer to the original 'In the beginning' – but the nearest they'll get is Greek. Echoes is all we ever get, the air shaken by speech, the seismograph. There's never a sign but in translation.

Still, if time began, it's always beginning somewhere, quite apart from nostalgic algebra.

> I gave my daughter a box of crayons.
> First she chewed it then she rattled it.
> This went on for quite some time.
> When she did put wax to paper
> she just did rhythm, cardiograms.

Note that none of the above groups could have been extrapolated from its predecessor. There's something miraculous about vegetable from mineral, birds budding from branches. A miracle, true, is that which no rational being can believe in. But then rational beings didn't deduce themselves from cognates in the trees. All they can do in this area is explain themselves away. Showing how something has evolved over time explains it in the etymological sense (it unfolds the thing origamically). It does not explain things in the common sense of saying why they're there. So why are we here? Wait a minute.

Words

What symmetry do we have in letters? numbers? words? This English alphabet (capital letters) has 6 letters without an axis of symmetry, 4 with rotational symmetry – three of them through 180 degrees, one complete, 3 others with two axes of bilateral symmetry, and the rest with one axis of bilateral symmetry: 2 diagonal, 4 horizontal and 7, like us, vertical. Of the digits, 2 have two axes of bilateral symmetry, 1 has a horizontal axis, 1 has full rotational symmetry and 1 rotates through 180 degrees into another. Not much of a pattern. In fact, the distribution is just about random, as though the idea were to get the maximum variety from simple signs, which seems practical.

Words: they are produced by symmetrical organs. The shapes those organs make – the cave of 'ae', the tube of 'oo', the closed gates of 'n', the glug of 'g' – are just as bilaterally symmetrical as us, but there is no symmetry at all in words, not even 'Malayalam': play it backwards, it doesn't sound the same. They're borne on breath, spoken in time, and can't be taken back. A word on time: it seems it was thinking about right and left that led Kant to say that space and time were intuitions. Blinkers, more like. Time is a syndrome quarks may not suffer from, but we do; like speech, it is not a palindrome. It's a fuite en avant, the devil in the driving mirror. Symmetry is a sign of ecstasy. Make love, 'the beast with two backs' (in the words of Othello's adviser) and that's another sinuous axis of it. Make love or, better still, play football! Since while the converse goes without saying, it must be emphasised here that thoughts about symmetry or any other activity are at best irrelevant to love-making; also, the rerouting of blood from the brain during intercourse is likely to have an adverse effect on thought. On the other hand, some consideration during your next match with Hamilton (NZ) Academicals ('the beast with two forwards') as to what your opposite number thinks your next move is going to be, and vice versa, might just improve your game. Symmetries, like axioms and the line-up, are for what is settled; the operative part is asymmetric. Some verse doesn't get as far as symmetry: there's only one team on the park, triumphant in its haletotic bardic breath. Some verse can't break out of symmetry, like two collusive teams whiling away 90 minutes. Some transcends it, though, like the human face. 'Soccer isn't a matter of life and death: it's much more important than that.'

Ports of Perception

If something is apprehended on its axis, if the axis is a port of perception, any symmetry it might have would not be directly perceived. You'll see the symmetry in the shape of a leaf, but not in its colour, because you're at the end of a beam that's undergone filtration and reflection in the leaf and in your eyes. You can feel (and hear some) symmetry in forces and objects, but not in their textures, since the axis is at the meeting of (say) fingertip and surface. The same applies to olfactory receptors and taste buds, where molecules join. There aren't symmetrical smells. And smell is intimate with taste. And taste, like speech, runs along the tongue, sweet at the tip, salt on the blade, boiled broccoli at the uvula.

Are we ourselves the axes of some further symmetry, drawn towards a moment of balance, strained and used by it till we have neither shape, nor humanity, nor name? If time were a fourth dimension, desire could be a sixth sense – but it doesn't get us closer than the other five to answering that question. What desire has it doesn't want: itself, this moment, part of me. It yaws like a compass needle when the lode is on a plane it can't turn to. I want to be this, to have that, but not to have been or be had; I want to go and do things, not be gone or done in; I want to stay, I don't want left behind. All the conjugations tell the same story: desire is centrifugal, contradictory, and as absolutely time-bound as speech. What I'm after is something that does with existence what poetry does with utterance: not reduce the world to symmetries but adumbrate the patterns we're in: it's more a prayer than a power game.

This spiel is mostly mineral, punctate, logical in its way. It's crystallising outwards from the word 'symmetry'. It's about to be twisted by the word.

Chirality

I can't believe that the spiral – the word itself suggests circle and parallel – isn't symmetrical. Find yourself a spiral staircase. There is a good one on Bridge Street in Glasgow, over the Glaswegian pub, I think. A steep flight of stairs from Nelson Street takes you to the circular floor of a cylindrical stairwell. A hanging stair winds widdershins up the wall. Stand at the top and look down. In fact, raise the building another ten floors to make the point quite clear. The banister spirals in towards the centre of the floor of the stairwell, though the staircase has a circular plan – which gives it infinite rotational or mirror symmetry – and in elevation, if we ignore the fact that this particular example levels out into a landing once in every full turn, it is a sine curve set on its side, which gives it two axes of symmetry for every floor it rises (one for each peak and trough of the sine curve).

You may object that I have found symmetry not in a spiral but in the plan and the elevation of a helix. Very good. What I have said is that the spiral can be analysed into two components that have symmetry. The same is true of other obvious examples: cyclones and snail shells. But before we return to specifics, a word on dimensions. For a long time I exercised my trivial imagination on quadrivial space. I tried to see what happened to a party of particles whizzing up and down the four axes (x, y, z and t) of length, breadth, depth and time. It's only this morning that I have finally realized that that's as pointless as trying to visualise quantities in their progress through a long division sum. Feyaman diagrams? I'll no more see a particle in there than I'd see the newscaster's scalp if I sawed the top off my TV (and I don't have one). To me, space is nothing and nothing doesn't have a shape, but I won't be bothered by the next physicist who tells me that space-time is curved: all he means is that his co-ordinate system is screwy. If he can live with that, so can I.

Dimensions

But there is still less to dimensions than meets the eye. I cannot visualise one dimension either. Judging from the problems that generations of Greek geometers had in deciding on the nature of the point – Zeno reduced it to the absurd but no-one quite reduced it to unity or set it at naught – there is no shame in that inability. John Burnet thought Leukippos had solved it with the atom, but then Burnet was writing when Rutherford (who visualised atoms as billiard balls) seemed to have done the same. Heisenberg seems to have worried at the same bone (wave or particle? verb or noun?). Worse still – put it down to stereoscopic vision if you like – I am not at all sure that I can see in two dimensions. A line always implies a space. I see nothing but surfaces and I assume, always, that there is depth to them. That is why the spiral is so obviously symmetrical. That is what painters play on: when a surface doesn't make sense the viewer looks into it. When that doesn't make sense either, stay cool: it's the twentieth century. The artist might just be making the point that I am making here: there is no point; don't trust appearances; don't trust realities either.

So if I can't see four dimensions, or one dimension or even two, then what is the point in talking of three? Dimensions are for graph paper. They set things straight: they put vision and dementia behind bars, which isn't always a bad thing, though always is a bad thing: somebody has to take a shillelagh to Occam's razor gang from time to time, and defend different interpretations of the world: a sycamore has one, morning glory has another, the black redstart has a third – to say nothing of barnacle geese, goose barnacles, beautiful hooktips etc. In other words, respect not only what divides one realm, one science from another (crystals have no pentagonal lattice while cinquefoil plants are common) but what distinguishes each creature from the next. Name them. I do not deny the use of categories: in learning a language, for example, paradigms help distinguish por from para in Spanish, and indicate when to use which aspect of a double imperfective verb in Russian. But there are so many exceptions to the rules, and flaws in the pattern of exceptions, that you have to choose eventually either language, languages, worn stone stairs, eroded reason, most irregular in the most used words, or the practice of weeding out linguistic illogicalities and ambiguities so you can express things more clearly, make do with clarity, and miss out on symmetries that don't add up (see 'Insomnia' below).

Mirrors

Symmetry round a vertical plane didn't exist before animals. And it wasn't confused before the invention of mirrors. Reflection in water distinguished opposites: up from down, sea from sky, root from branch, sun from seed; reflection in the glass compared and confused similarities: right and left, and wrong; dexterous, gauche and sinister. They can be both similar and opposite, things of the heart, hope and despair. The intimate but unseen schism between handedness and heartedness, heart and hand, and the way that opposites rotate into similes, unsettle. There's a flat contradiction between two senses, sight and touch. Mirror imagery is not to be taken at face value.

Insomnia

The moon in the bureau mirror
looks out a million miles
(and perhaps with pride, at herself,
but she never, never smiles)
far and away beyond sleep, or
perhaps she's a daytime sleeper.

By the Universe deserted,
she'd tell it to go to hell,
and she'd find a body of water,
or a mirror, on which to dwell.
So wrap up care in a cobweb
and drop it down the well

into that world inverted
where left is always right,
where the shadows are really the body,
where we stay awake all night,
where the heavens are shallow as the sea
is now deep, and you love me.

Elizabeth Bishop

Writing is an up-and-down reflection: I think things up and write them down, and there is no more danger of mistaking the words for the world (though it happens), than of taking sea for sky. The cinema, though, is a back-to-front reflection, a mirror image, and film very often is mistaken for life.

The mirror is neither me nor you.
The word is both of us.
So how were we divided?

We could start with two sets of 23 chromosomes, join them up, and follow cell division till it produce up and down, right and left, and another creature with another set of 23 to offer, but that's not really the beginning. I'll take another story. Adam was divided from the earth, Eve from Adam, settler from nomad, hairy Esau from gentle Jacob, builder from planner. Babel! The ziggurat, helical sign of division. With that kind of history between us, any communication is fraught. Clarity isn't the most important quality here, it's charity, trust that ambiguities are honest and illogicalities are true. It's an interpersonal thing and the only important axis of symmetry is the page.

I turned to symmetry hoping for help
in staking out my heart, but it's the knotted
cord itself that sets the measure.
'Queue que soit la fécondité d'une méthode,
son office est surtout de consolidation
et, si l'on vent, de prolongement,
mais sur un terrain préalablement fixé.
Elle met en ordre l'acquis et, ce faisant,
comble les lacunes et exploite les percées,
mais elle n'inaugure rien d'essentiellement neuf'

Robert Blanche, *L'Axiomatique*

Mozart kicked away the ladder Bach had come up by, and I've had enough of broken chords and scales. There's one way and one way only to go about it: find an angel and pick a fight.

REVIEWS

MARK COUSINS

RICHARD BURTON

MICHAEL NEWTON

Petrolio Notice

MARK COUSINS

Pier Paolo Pasolini's films are amongst the least mannered in all of cinema. They make their meanings through archaic, Piero della Francesca imagery. His poems find their unforgettable intensities through the devotional language of prayer.

His three novels, however, have never seemed like major achievements to me. *Ragazzi di vita* (1955), *Una vita violenta* (1959) and *A Dream of Something* (1962) are paradoxical, wannabe films, schematic, heavy, toiling to be visual. They always, in my estimation, ranked third in the Pasolini canon, after the poems and the films.

Now a bundle of papers found on the desk of the writer and film maker, shortly after his death, and carefully published by Secker and Warburg under the title *Petrolio*, makes it look like Pasolini might have had a great novel in him.

Petrolio begins exquisitely with Carlo, its main character, standing on the balcony of an apartment. We are in the month of May 1960, a time when 'Neo-capitalism was the term of a culture still too privileged to change the feel of reality'. Carlo falls to what seems to be his death and, in a passage worthy of Ovid, becomes two people: Carlo the first, a bourgeois oil company worker whose addiction to power is a metaphor for fascism, and Carlo the second, who lusts for bodies, who becomes a woman, whose imagination is exclusively erotic.

These historical and dialectical concerns are familiar Pasolini themes. What makes *Petrolio* more significant than author's previous novels is the complex interiority of his character. Pasolini has realised that novels can do things that films can't. He engages with the movements of minds here rather than the 'stupendous' worship of the way the world looks.

As *Petrolio* comprises 521 typed pages of notes, a 'Project Note', a plot outline, almost completed chapters, clear revisions in coloured ink and a long letter to Alberto Moravia asking advice about the prose style used, and as everything is published, it is collage-like and post modern in a way that its author might well have detested. Its comments on itself, its direct address to the reader, its markings out and intended revisions, are fascinating, like Leonardo da Vinci's pentimenti, or the X-ray pictures of a Caravaggio. It is impossible to say whether revisions and editing might have excised or made readable some of the incredible industrial and sexual longeurs: there are complex accounts of Italian business history which are like paste-ins from a text book, and one long account of 30 consecutive fellatios is either appallingly weak writing or a calculated distancing device.

Petrolio makes you feel closer to Pasolini than anything since his documentary *Seeking Locations in Palestine for the Film "The Gospel According to St Matthew"*

Abandoned Wine: Chinese Writing of Today 2
Edited by Henry Y. H. Zhao and John Cayley
Wellsweep, 1997, 1 Grove End House, 150 Highgate Road, London NW5 1PD
ISBN 0 948454 24 5 p/b 320pp £8.95

RICHARD BURTON

This is the second biennial anthology of works selected by Chinese writers and critics from *Today*, a suppressed Chinese literary journal that was re-launched in 1990 from Sweden. The book's 14 works of fiction, 9 essays, 36 poems, and Foreword by Gary Snyder provide an essential window into Chinese literature, but few of the 314 pages did not delight me simply as 'a good read'.

Many of the Chinese writers live, or have lived, in Europe or America, so much of the writing is unsurprisingly cosmopolitan: inspired by a Chinese porcelain bowl, Lee Yu delightfully interwines memories of his grandmother's favourite bowl with Proust's recollections of a cup of lime flower tea; a love of western literature is manifested by Zhang Zao in his interview with Gennadi Aigi, and by Chen Jinhua in 'Swan by an endless stream' (a title based on Baudelaire and Poe) which celebrates the twenty-fifth anniversary of the death of Zhu Yulin, poet, translator and enthusiast for Pushkin, Heine, Whitman ...: 'We could all argue vociferously about *Anna Karenina,* as if we could never exhaust its spirit, but if the topic of conversation turned to the contemporary Chinese literature world [i.e. 1966-8], there was only silence and sighing, as though we had encountered a stretch of wasteland.' Yet the perception of being in the shadow of western literature can bring problems and anxieties, and these are brilliantly explored in an essay by Huang Ziping.

Cultures also meet (British, Tibetan, Chinese, Indian) in Ge Fei's story of Younghusband's military expedition into Tibet in 1903-4. Here the dangers of fictionalizing history are countered by obvious fantasy and unknowable detail. (Contemporary accounts differ greatly, but agree that Younghusband's countrymen disapproved of the slaughter.) Of course, there are purely Chinese tales too – of comedy, classical scholarship and, above all, imagination.

Of the poems, I like many more than I expect of such collections. Huang Ziping cautions against applying western labels to Chinese literature, so I offer only 'broadly modernist' and, for some poems, 'challengingly kaleidoscopic'. Let the poetry speak for itself through these re-assembled shards: *Why* Today? / *Words awaken, lift their skirts, face each other, / all swirling under a demon's tongue. / Words take off and tumble / and / the earth pricks up its ears. / The overlapping of East and West / becomes a brilliant moment, / a peacock stone, / the tail of language on which the shrieks of the peacock grow. / If you disappear into this book, / the phrases that I have stored up / – this / torn collection of poetry / hung with icicles of fantasy – / become sentences for you / Push through the crowd and you can enter.*

Wellsweep (London) has published collections of poems by two of the poets in *Abandoned Wine,* namely Duo Duo (*Statements*, 1989) and Yang Lian (*Non-Person Singular*, 1994 – see *Edinburgh Review* 95 – and *Where the Sea Stands Still*, 1995). It is the only UK press to specialize in Chinese literary translation and is establishing an important reputation in the field of classical and modern Chinese poetry and prose.

The Identity of the Scottish Nation
William Ferguson
1998, Edinburgh: Edinburgh University Press
ISBN 0 7486 1071 5.

MICHAEL NEWTON

That famous English philologist and author J. R. R. Tolkien once said 'History often resembles "Myth", because they are both ultimately made of the same stuff.' Because all history is shaped by the perspectives of the people who write it and by the biases of the age in which it is written, it is inevitable that history is coloured by a variety of lenses. It is the heroic quest of William Ferguson's latest book to explore Scottish Historiography, to discuss the dominant ideological forces and issues in Scottish culture through time and the impact that these have had upon the articulation of Scottish history and identity. This is a masterly tour de force that no one can afford to miss, full of revelations that should dispel many of the current myths that obscure Scottish history.

Ferguson, an Honorary Fellow and former lecturer in the Scottish History Department of Edinburgh University, begins with the earliest evidence of the formation of Gaelic identity and origin legends, particularly as surviving in medieval Irish literature. The frequent references to Irish Gaeldom, as he notes, will not be pleasing to many in Scotland: 'In truth, the desire to minimise the Irish dimension runs like a refrain through many modern discussions of Scottish identity ...' (p. 45). Still, he reminds us that the facts of history necessarily require the Irish connection:

> Indeed, the outstanding fact is that most of the main racial stocks from which the early Scottish nation evolved furnished nothing of any real substance of later arguments about Scottish national origin or identity ... The origin of the Scottish nation is not in any detectable measure Pictish, British, Anglian or Norse, as the Declaration of Arbroath made very clear: Scottish identity clearly and evidently evolves from the Gaelic tradition of Ireland as received, developed and modified in Scotland. (pp. 13, 45)

The development of Scottish historical research was often fuelled by political controversy. Although he suggests that the Gaels of Dál Riada may have taken an early form of the Gaidel Glas origin legend with them to Scotland, the expansionism of Edward I of England required an ideological response in terms of the national origin legend. Edward, for his part, justified his subjugation of Scotland by invoking the legendary Brutus in Geoffrey of Monmouth. The ancient origin legend of the Scots, reflecting the prevailing Gaelic ethos of the kingdom, opened the famous Declaration of Arbroath as evidence of the Scots' separate ethnicity and indomitable nature.

The Kingdom of Scotland had a

decidedly marked advantage over England in this contest: whereas there were at least two ethnic discontinuities in the English kingship – the Celtic inheritors of Brutus' throne had been conquered and dispossessed by Anglo-Saxons and then by Normans – the kings of Scotland could trace their pedigree right back to the Dál Riadan kings. It is important to remember that kingship itself was central to the idea of a *king*dom, and was a focus and embodiment of the ideals and identity of that nation. It was because of such principles that Scottish King Lists were compiled and manipulated, and became the source of bitter historical contention for centuries to come.

The religious controversies that began in the Reformation and continued to flare up periodically into the eighteenth century also channeled energies into developing historical studies. Those wishing either to defend or attack the new presbyterian order went to historical sources to justify their stance by seeking ancient precedents, although these pioneer scholars employed far more creativity than objectivity in their writing. Still, these heated disputes ignited the efforts to find and interpret early historical sources, and in England led to the founding of Anglo-Saxon Studies.

This historical quest not only delves into historiography but into the History of Ideas in Europe. As a Celticist, I particularly enjoyed Ferguson's discussion about the foundations of Celtic Studies, which not only resulted from the aforementioned religious and political debates but also from antiquarianism, primitivism, the search for European origins and the row over Macpherson's Ossian. Whereas Anglo-Saxon Studies enjoyed a privileged status in the romantic nationalism that built the English nation, Celtic Studies, until the twentieth century, has lacked the patronage and stability needed to bring the field to maturity. Indeed, Ferguson reminds us that the foundation of Celtic Studies was laid by George Buchanan in the sixteenth century, whose identification of the Pictish language as Celtic with closer affinity to Gaulish than Brittonic is the accepted opinion of modern scholars. Had his political opinions not brought disapproval on his writings altogether, Scottish historical studies might have had a better head start.

The development of Celtic Studies, especially in a Scottish context, has suffered setbacks and regressions time and time again in a hostile cultural and political environment. Union with England encouraged the glorification of Anglo-Teutons and the denigration of Celts. The prejudice against Ireland in particular pressured generations of scholars to invent an ancient Scottish history which avoided mention of this 'inferior race' and acknowledgement of their role in building the nation. It is on account of these fears and biases that the Picts have been the ideological football of Scottish atavists, continually reinvented by those with particular agendas. Ferguson recounts the various interpretations of the Picts as Britons, Gaels, Goths and 'mystery people' and the reasons for these recreations.

One of the subtexts in the book is the attempt to address a number of modern misconceptions about Scottish history and identity. In particular, Ferguson debunks the many fallacies of Hugh Trevor-Roper, whose zeal for disparaging and misrepresenting realities of Scottish culture and history is matched by his lack of knowledge about them. Ferguson in particular takes the time to focus on the Ossianic debate and the illumination which Gaelic sources shed on the issue. Not only were the Fenian lays paramount in the oral tradition of the Highlands into the present century, but Macpherson was only one in a long line who employed the elements of Ossianic poetry for an English speaking audience.

Ferguson only briefly touches upon Scottish identity in the present century, noting at it has survived despite attempts at assimilation and that Scottish nationalism has a positive role to play in the reintegration of the nation's identity. It may be taken as an unstated corollary of Ferguson's analysis that the break-down of an Anglo-centric hegemony and the self-confident blossoming of Irish culture at the present time could dispel the divisive forces which have inhibited Scotland's acknowledgement of its Gaelic origins and its self- realisation.

There are a few quibbles that a Celticist might voice about this book. In attempting to redress the lack of esteem given to Scottish Gaelic poetry, Ferguson rightly points out that what survives from the seventeenth century shows remarkable vigour and beauty worthy of much greater attention. It may be overcompensation to suggest that it overshadows other Celtic poetry of the era, however. In discussing the *Lebor Gabála*, a more recent authority than the now outdated T. F. O' Rahilly needs to be consulted. Such details, however, do not diminish the success of Ferguson's historic quest.

Contributors

John Burnside is an award-winning poet, novelist and writer of short stories, born in Dunfermline and now living in Fife after many years in England.

Regi Claire (formerly Yvonne Claire) is Swiss and now lives in Edinburgh with her husband and their dog. She received an SAC Writers' Bursary in 1997. Her first collection of stories, *Inside – Outside* has recently been published. 'Kalsang's Brother' is her third piece to be published in *ER*.

Peter Constantine is a New York-based translator from Afrikaans, German, Modern Greek and the ethnic minority languages of Greece. He is the translator of *Thomas Mann – Six Early Stories* and the author of many books on Japanese, Indonesian and Korean culture.

Gerrie Fellows is a New Zealand-born poet and writer, now based in Scotland. She is the author of *Technologies and Other Poems* (Polygon) and has worked as a Writing Fellow with Renfrew District Libraries and as a writing tutor with Glasgow University.

Kaarina Hollo is based in the Department of Celtic Languages and Literatures at Harvard University.

Brian Holton was born in 1949 in Galashiels and describes himself as a jobbing sinologist, a writer and translator who has taught Chinese at the universities of Edinburgh and Durham.

Stuart Hood has translated two of Pasolini's novels, *Theorem* and *A Dream of Something*, as well as his *Lutheran Letters* and *Volume 1* of his correspondence. He interpreted for Dario Fo in performances of *Mistero Buffo* at the Riverside Theatre in London and in the Edinburgh Festival. His novel *A Storm from Paradise* won the Saltire prize in 1985, whilst in *Carlino* he described his experiences as an escaped POW in Italy and his life with the peasants and partisans.

Coral Hull was born in Paddington, New South Wales, Australia in 1965. She is a full time writer and a member of the Field Naturalists Club of Victoria and The Australian Society of Authors; and is an animal rights advocate and Director of Animal Watch Australia. She has published four books with Penguin Books Australia and her work has appeared in literary magazines in the USA, Canada, Australia and the UK.

Alexander Hutchison is a poet and translator in Scots and English, author of *Four Poems in Broadside* (Rampant Lions), *Deep-Tap Tree* (University of Massachusetts), *The Mooncalf* (Galliard), *Carbuncle's Culinary* (MMMM) and *Epitaph for a Butcher* (Akros).

Peter McCarey is a writer and translator who lives in Geneva. He has been published extensively in literary magazines and his books include *Hugh MacDiarmid and the Russians*, *Town Shanties* and *The Devil in the Driving Mirror.*

Barbara Nicgriogair is a poet based in Glasgow. She describes herself as a 'langscape artist' and eternal student and works for Her Majesty's Stationery Office.

Mario Relich is a writer and translator, based in Edinburgh.

Carla Sassi is a writer and translator, based in Trieste.

Ziranna Zateli is a Greek novelist and short story writer.

Edinburgh Review

SUBMISSIONS

We are pleased to receive submissions of original fiction, poetry and articles provided they are accompanied by a stamped addressed envelope or International Reply Coupons – please note that if postage is not included then manuscripts cannot be returned. It is greatly appreciated if contributors are able to supply, along with a paper copy of their submission, a disk in a format readable in Word 7.

The *Review* receives a large number of submissions, and we aim to reach a decision on all material within three months.

Contributors are asked to follow the guidelines set out below:

Length
Typescripts should not exceed 6,000 words.

Presentation
Material should be clearly typed and double-spaced on one side of A4 paper. Two copies should be submitted. Section headings should be in upper and lower case and centred; sub-section headings should be underlined. Single quotation marks should be used for main quotations, double for any quotes within the main quotation. Quotations of more than forty words should be indented. Foreign words (except proper names) should be underlined. Dates should be in the format of 23 July 1945, the 1940s, 1952-6, numerals up to ninety-nine should be spelt out, but all other numbers given in figures, e.g. 14-18 per cent; titles and initials of institutions or countries should be given without full stops: Dr, USA, COSLA, UNESCO etc.

Illustrations
These should be placed at the end of the article, each on a separate sheet of paper together with the relevant caption, and numbered. The number should also be placed in the margin of the text to indicate where the illustration is to appear. Sources should be acknowledged.

Notes
These should be kept to an absolute minimum, and where possible footnotes should be avoided, with sources appearing in parentheses within the main body of the text. Where footnotes are unavoidable they should be double-spaced, numbered consecutively, and placed together at the end of the text.

Copyright
It is the responsibility of the author to obtain written permission to reprint any previously published material in copyright.

In the case of acceptance for publication, the author will be notified of the fee offered and of any suggested major changes to the text. The editors reserve the right to make minor stylistic revisions. Authors will normally receive proofs, at which stage only typographical or factual errors can be corrected. Contributors will receive one complimentary copy of the issue in which their material appears.

Sophy Dale – Editor
Edinburgh Review
22a Buccleuch Place, Edinburgh EH8 9LN
Tel/Fax: 0131 651 1415 e-mail: eliedrevp@srv0.arts.ed.ac.uk

Issue 100
Edinburgh Review

Edinburgh Review's hundredth issue will be published to coincide with the run-up to the elections for the new Scottish parliament and will take as its theme the intersections between politics, culture and nationhood in Scotland. Including new writing from Alan Warner, Edwin Morgan, John Burnside, Tom Leonard and Duncan McLean; interviews with A.L. Kennedy and Janice Galloway; and features on the politics of Scottish theatre; Gordon Legge on the New Beat Generation of Scottish writers; the new parliament building assessed as part of a tradition of Scottish democratic assemblies; W.N. Herbert on Hugh MacDiarmid and Patrick Geddes; and much, much more... this issue of *Edinburgh Review* is a feast of the best in contemporary writing, and an opportunity to take time out from the politicians' sound-bites to reflect upon the implications of the shift in Scotland's national status both for Scotland's writers and for its readers. Forming a complement to Issue 99's international scope, Issue 100 sees the magazine with an unusually Scotland-centred focus, since this particular moment in time seems to demand a real attempt to review Scotland's changing situation. The hope is that in the local will be found the universal, and that a thorough assessment of the pros and cons of Scotland's changing status will have implications which may find echoes elsewhere.